Interfaith Ministry Handbook

Prayers, Readings and Other Resources
for Pastoral Settings

Compiled by
Matt Sanders

Luke 10:27

Love the Lord your God
with all your heart, and with all your soul,
and with all your strength, and with all your mind,
and Love your neighbor
as yourself.

Apocryphile Press
1700 Shattuck Ave #81
Berkeley, CA 94709
www.apocryphile.org

ISBN 9781940671697

The Chaplain's Covenant

Written by Gregory A. Perry.
Distributed by the Association of
Professional Chaplains. Used by permission.

I do solemnly affirm by the One
   who is Creator and Sustainer of life:
That I will be faithful to my calling,
   the profession of chaplaincy;
That I will respect the religious and spiritual traditions
   of my patients, colleagues, and neighbors,
   as well as my own;
That I will lead my life and practice the art of ministry
   in an honorable and ethical manner;
That into whatsoever circumstances I shall enter,
   it shall be for the well-being
   of the people entrusted to my care;
That I will utilize the authority of the pastoral office
   for the purpose of furthering
   the unfolding work of God,
   providing opportunity for all
   to receive the welcome afforded by grace;
That I will respect the confidentiality
   of those who put their trust in me;
That I will promote peace among all people,
   valuing our diverse gifts,
   and celebrating our common origins.
With the One who is Creator and Sustainer of life,
   and with my colleagues in the profession of chaplaincy,
   I solemnly and freely make this covenant.

CONTENTS

Part Three: Prayers for
Specific Needs in a Hospital Setting

Part Four: Biblical Reources: Topical Listings

Part Five: Songs

Part Six: Other Resources

PART I

PRAYERS & READINGS FROM THE WORLD RELIGIONS, 12-STEP, & MISC

Jewish Prayers & Scriptures

The Priestly Blessing
Num 6:24-26 (RSV)

The Lord bless you and keep you.
The Lord make his face to shine upon you
    and be gracious to you.
The Lord lift up his countenance upon you
    and grant you peace! Amen.

On the Importance of Reciting Scripture
Talmud

"Though a person has recited the *Sh'ma* in the synagogue, it is a religious act to recite it again upon one's bed... Abaye says: Even a scholar should recite one verse of supplication, as for example, "Into Your hand I commit my spirit; You have redeemed me, O Lord, God of truth."

(Quote from the Talmud, quoted in Fountain of Life, compiled by Rabbi Arthur A. Chiel and Rabbi Edward T. Sandrow, The Rabbinical Assembly, New York, 1975, p.12. www.ktav.com.)

Sh'ma Yisrael
Deuteronomy 6:4-9 (RSV)

Sh'ma Yisra'el Eloheinu Adonai Ehad.

Hear, O Israel: The Lord our God is one Lord;

And you shall love the Lord your God with all your heart, and with all your soul, and with all your might.

And these words which I command you this day shall be upon your heart; and you shall teach them diligently to your children, and shall talk of them when you sit in your house, and when you walk by the way, and when you lie down, and when you rise. And you shall bind them as a sign upon your hand, and they shall be as frontlets between your eyes. And you shall write them on the doorposts of your house and on your gates.

1 Sam 3:10 (NIV)

The LORD came and stood there, calling as at the other times, "Samuel! Samuel!"

Then Samuel said, "Speak, for your servant is listening."

Neh 8:10 (NIV)

Do not grieve, for the joy of the LORD is your strength.

Psalm 5:1-5a, 7-8a, 11-12 (NIV)
(Listen to my cry. Sing for joy in the Lord.)

Give ear to my words, O Lord, consider my sighing. Listen to my cry for help, my King and my God, for to you I pray. In the morning, O Lord, you hear my voice; in the morning I lay my requests before you and wait in expectation.

You are not a God who takes pleasure in evil; with you the wicked cannot dwell. The arrogant cannot stand in your presence...

But I, by your great mercy, will come into your house; in reverence will I bow down toward your holy temple. Lead me, O Lord, in your righteousness...

...(L)et all who take refuge in you be glad; let them ever sing for joy. Spread your protection over them, that those who love your name may rejoice in you. For surely, O Lord, you bless the righteous; you surround them with your favor as with a shield.

Psalm 23 (KJV)
(The Lord is my Shepherd)

The Lord is my shepherd; I shall not want. He maketh me to lie down in green pastures; he leadeth me beside the still waters. He restoreth my soul; he leadeth me in the paths of righteousness for his name's sake.

Yea, though I walk through the valley of the shadow of death, I will fear no evil: for thou art with me; thy rod and thy staff they comfort me.

Thou preparest a table before me in the presence of mine enemies; thou anointest my head with oil; my cup runneth over.

Surely goodness and mercy shall follow me all the days of my life; and I will dwell in the house of the Lord for ever.

Psalm 34:1-12, 17-18 (NIV)
(I will bless the Lord at all times)

I will extol the Lord at all times; his praise will always be on my lips. My soul will boast in the Lord; let the afflicted hear and rejoice. Glorify the Lord with me; let us exalt his name together.

I sought the Lord, and he answered me; he delivered me from all my fears. Those who look to him are radiant; their faces are never covered with shame.

This poor man called, and the Lord heard him; he saved him out of all his troubles. The angel of the Lord encamps around those who fear him, and he delivers him.

Taste and see that the Lord is good, blessed is the man who takes refuge in him. Fear the Lord, you his saints, for those who fear him lack nothing. The lions may grow weak and hungry, but those who seek the Lord lack no good thing. Come, my children, listen to me; I will teach you the fear of the Lord. Whoever of you loves life and desires to see many good days, keep your tongue from evil and your lips from speaking lies. Turn from evil and do good; seek peace and pursue it.

The righteous cry out, and the Lord hears them; he delivers them from all their troubles. The Lord is close to the brokenhearted and save those who are crushed in spirit.

Psalm 37:3-6 (NIV)
(Trust in the Lord)

Trust in the Lord and do good; dwell in the land and enjoy safe pasture. Delight yourself in the Lord and he will give you the desires of your heart.

Commit your way to the Lord; trust in him and he will do this: he will make your righteousness shine like the dawn, the justice of your cause like the noonday sun.

Pslam 42:1-3, 5-6a, 7-9, 11 (NRSV)
(When depressed: As the deer pants for streams)

As a deer longs for flowing streams, so my soul longs for you, O God. My soul thirsts for God, for the living God. When shall I come and behold the face of God? My tears have been my food day and night, while people say to me continually, "Where is your God?"

Why are you cast down, O my soul, and why are you disquieted within me? Hope in God; for I shall again praise him, my help and my God.

My soul is downcast within me; therefore I will remember you from the land of Jordan... Deep calls to deep at the thunder of your cataracts; all your waves and your billows have gone over me.

By day the Lord commands his steadfast love, and at night his song is with me, a prayer to the God of my life. I say to God, my rock, "Why have you forgotten me? Why must I walk about mournfully because the enemy oppresses me?"

Why are you cast down, O my soul, and why are you disquieted within me? Hope in God; for I shall again praise him, my help and my God.

Psalm 46:1 (KJV)

God is our refuge and strength, a very present help in trouble.

Psalm 46:10 (RSV)

Be still and know that I am God.
Be still and know that I am.
Be still and know.
Be still.
Be.

(Note: Pause between each line and breathe calmly. You may also wish to imagine a bell being rung between each line. This breathing or bell brings you to the present moment.)

Psalm 63:2-9
(My soul thirsts. I cling to you.)

O God, you are my God—for you I long! For you my body yearns; for you my soul thirsts. Like a land parched, lifeless, and without water.

So I look to you in the sanctuary to see your power and glory. For your love is better than life; my lips offer you worship! I will bless you as long as I live; I will lift up my hands, calling on your name. My soul shall savor the rich banquet of praise, with joyous lips my mouth shall honor you.

As I lie in bed I remember you, through the night watches I will recall that you indeed are my help, and in the shadow of your wings I shout for joy. My soul clings fast to you; your right hand upholds me.

Psalm 91:1-6, 9-16 (NIV)
(When anxious: Fear not. Angels will guard you.)

He who dwells in the shelter of the Most High will rest in the shadow of the Almighty. I will say of the Lord, "He is my refuge and my fortress, my God in whom I trust."

Surely he will save you from the fowler's snare and from the deadly pestilence. He will cover you with his feathers, and under his wings you will find refuge; his faithfulness will be your shield and rampart. You will not fear the terror of the night, nor the arrow that flies by day, nor the pestilence that stalks in the darkness, nor the plague that destroys at midday. ...

If you make the Most High your dwelling—even the Lord, who is my refuge—then no harm will befall you, no disaster will come near your tent. For he will command his angels concerning you to guard you in all your ways; they will lift you up in their hands, so that you will not strike your foot against a stone.

You will tread upon the lion and the cobra; you will trample the great lion and the serpent.

The Lord says, "Because he loves me, I will rescue him, for he acknowledges my name. He will call upon me, and I will answer him; I will be with him in trouble, I will deliver him and honor him. With long life will I satisfy him and show him my salvation."

Psalm 100 (NIV)
(Make a joyful noise)

Shout for joy to the Lord, all you earth. Worship the Lord with gladness; come before him with joyful songs. Know that the Lord is God. It is he who made us, and we are his; we are his people, the sheep of his pasture.

Enter his gates with thanksgiving and his courts with praise; give thanks to him and praise his name. For the Lord is good and his love endures forever; his faithfulness continues through all generations.

Psalm 118:24 (NIV)

This is the day the Lord has made; let us rejoice and be glad in it!

Psalm 118:29

Give thanks to the Lord for he is good; his love is everlasting.

Psalm 119:105 (KJV)

Thy word is a lamp unto my feet and a light unto my path.

Psalm 119:106 (NIV)

I have taken an oath and confirmed it, that I will follow your righteous laws.

Psalm 121:1-3, 5-8 (NRSV)

(Protection. According to the Jewish Study Bible of the Jewish Publication Society, "In many contemporary Jewish communities [this psalm] is recited at times of trouble as a way of offering comfort and assurance.")

I lift up my eyes to the hills— from where does my help come? My help comes from the Lord, who made heaven and earth.

He will not let your foot be moved; he who keeps you will not slumber... The Lord is your keeper; the Lord is your shade at your right hand. The sun shall not strike you by day, nor the moon by night.

The Lord will keep you from all evil — he will keep your life. The Lord will keep your going out and your coming in from this time on and forevermore.

Psalm 139:1-2, 3b, 5-6, 13-15a, 23-24 (NIV)
(You have formed me)

O Lord, you have searched me and you know me. You know when I sit and when I rise; you perceive my thoughts from afar...you are familiar with all my ways.

You hem me in — behind and before; you have laid your hand upon me. Such knowledge is too wonderful for me, too lofty for me to attain. ...

For you created my inmost being, you knit me together in my mother's womb. I praise you because I am fearfully and wonderfully made; your works are wonderful, I know that full well. My frame was not hidden from you when I was made in the secret place.

...Search me, O God, and know my heart; test me and know my anxious thoughts. See if there is any offensive way in me, and lead me in the way everlasting.

Proverbs 3:5-6 (NIV)

Trust in the Lord with all your heart, and lean not on your own understanding; in all your ways acknowledge him and he will make your paths straight.

Proverbs 17:22 (AMP)

A cheerful heart is good medicine, but low spirits sap a person's strength.

A happy heart is good medicine, *and* a cheerful mind works healing, but a broken spirit dries up the bones.

Ecclesiastes 3:1-8 (RSV)

For everything there is a season, and a time for every matter under heaven:

a time to be born, and a time to die;
a time to plant and a time to pluck up what is planted;
a time to kill and a time to heal;
a time to break down, and a time to build up;
a time to weep, and a time to laugh;
a time to mourn, and a time to dance;
a time to cast away stones,
and a time to gather stones together;
a time to embrace,
and a time to refrain from embracing;
a time to seek, and a time to lose;
a time to keep, and a time to cast away;
a time to rend, and a time to sew;
a time to keep silence, and a time to speak;
a time to love, and a time to hate;
a time for war, and a time of peace.

Isaiah 40:28-31 (NIV)
(On eagles wings)

Do you not know? Have you not heard? The LORD is the everlasting God, the Creator of the ends of the earth. He will not grow tired or weary, and his understanding no one can fathom.

He gives strength to the weary and increases the power of the weak. Even youths grow tired and weary, and young men stumble and fall; but those who hope in the LORD will renew their strength. They will soar on wings like eagles; they will run and not grow weary, they will walk and not be faint.

Jeremiah 29:11 (NIV)

"For I know the plans I have for you," declares the Lord, "Plans to prosper you and not to harm you, plans to give you hope and a future."

— MISC. JEWISH PRAYERS —

Jewish Prayer for Healing

May the one who blessed our ancestors—Abraham, Isaac and Jacob, Sarah, Rebecca, Rachel and Leah— bless and heal those who are ill [names].

May the Blessed Holy One be filled with compassion for their health to be restored and their strength to be revived. May God swiftly send them a complete renewal of body and spirit; and let us say, Amen.

May the Source of strength who blessed the ones before us, help us find the courage to make our lives a blessing, and let us say, Amen.

Bless those in need of healing with *r'fuah sh'leimah*, the renewal of body, the renewal of spirit; and let us say, Amen.

Blessing for Healing

El na refana la. = God, please heal her. *(la=her)*
El na refana lo. = God, please heal him. *(lo=him)*

Blessing for Healing: May God Heal You

(*For physical and spiritual healing. Can be said with laying on of hands. From* Talking to God, *Naomi Levy, p. 119.*)

May God heal you, body and soul.
May your pain cease;
May your strength increase;
May your fears be released;
May blessings, love and joy surround you. Amen.

Surrender Not to Sorrow
Ben Sira (Sirach) 30:21-25

Surrender not to sorrow, and stumble not in distress. A hopeful heart helps to keep you alive, and joy adds length of days. Relax yourself, soothe your heart, and banish anxiety. For sorrow and anxiety have destroyed many lives; they lead to no advantage. Envy and anger shorten one's life, and anxiety brings old age before its time. A person with a hopeful heart, those who are cheerful and merry at table, will develop a good appetite and benefit from their food.

(Source: Ecclesiasticus, or The Wisdom of Jesus Son of Sirach, from the Apocrypha or Deuterocanonical Scriptures. Vs 21-24 taken from Fountain of Life, compiled by Rabbi Arthur A. Chiel and Rabbi Edward T. Sandrow, The Rabbinical Assembly, New York, 1975, p.24. www.ktav.com. Vs 25 is a compilation paraphrase by Matt Sanders from this source and Holy Bible:New Revised Standard Version With Apocrypha.)

The following prayers are from compilation by Hana Matt, Judaism professor at The Chaplaincy Institute in Berkeley, CA, 2009:

Blessing & Praising God

1. *(To be said or sung every morning upon waking and opening one's eyes.)*
Modah ani lefanekha, ruah hai ve-qayam.=
I thank You in Your Presence, Spirit of Life enduring.
Elohai neshama sheh natata bi, tehora he.
My God, the soul you've given me, it is pure.

2. *Gam ki elekh be gay tsal mavet. Lo ira ra.*
   Yea, though I walk through the valley of the shadow
   of death, I will fear no evil. For you are with me.

3. *Min ha-meytsar (2x),*
   karati Yah. Ananee (2x)
   ba-merhav Yah.
   From constriction (2x)
   I called to God. God answered (2x)
   with spaciousness.

4. *Adonai li ve-lo ira ra.*
   God is with me, and I will not fear.

*(This is used as a meditation and deep breathing practice.
"God is with me" is said on the inhale, "I will not fear" on the
exhale.)*

Jewish Thanksgiving Blessing

[Individual recites:]
Baruch atah, Adonai Eloheinu
Melech haolam, sheg'malanu kol tov.
   Blessed are you, Adonai our God,
   Sovereign of the universe,
   who has bestowed every goodness upon us.
[Congregation responds:]
Amen. Mi sheg'malchem kol tov,
Hu yigmolchem kol tov. Selah.
   Amen. May the One
   who has bestowed goodness upon us
   continue to bestow every goodness upon us forever.

El Malei Rachamin
God, Filled with Mercy

(A prayer when remembering the dead.
Translation from Kol Haneshama)

God, filled with mercy, dwelling in the heavens' heights, bring proper rest beneath the wings of your *Shekhinah*, amid the ranks of the holy and the pure, illuminating like the brilliance of the skies the souls of our beloved and our blameless who went to the eternal place of rest. May you, who are the source of mercy, shelter them beneath your wings eternally, and bind their souls among the living, that they may rest in peace. And let us say: Amen.

On Recovery From Illness

Ba-rukh a-tah Adonai sho-may-a t'fi-lah.
Praised be You, O Lord who hears prayer.

Ba-rukh a-tah Adonai ro-fay cho-lim.
Praised be You, O Lord who heals the sick.

(Source: Fountain of Life, compiled by Rabbi Arthur A. Chiel and Rabbi Edward T. Sandrow, The Rabbinical Assembly, New York, 1975, p.18. www.ktav.com.)

Forgiveness & Prayer

During a terrible drought in ancient Israel in the 2nd century, the community was preparing to offer a prayer for rain. Even the powerful, pious scholar, Rabbi Eliezer, was unable to offer an effective prayer. Then suddenly Rabbi Akiva jumped up and cried aloud: "*Avinu Malkeinu* (Our Father, our King), there is no other sovereign but

You. *Avinu Malkeinu* (Our Father, our King), do with us for your name's sake."

Immediately the rains began to pour. "(I)t was said that God was more willing to hear Rabbi Akiva's prayer because he was able to forgive those who wronged him."

(From a transcript of a talk originally delivered at Temple Beth Sholom, San Leandro, 2009, by Linda Hirschhorn. Source: www.LindaHirschhorn.com . Note: Avinu=our Father, Malkeinu= our King.)

Visions of Love

(Source: Fountain of Life, compiled by Rabbi Arthur A. Chiel and Rabbi Edward T. Sandrow, The Rabbinical Assembly, New York, 1975, p.25. www.ktav.com.)

O God of peace, we seek rest for our spirits, and light for our thoughts. We bring our work to be sanctified, our wounds to be healed, our sins to be forgiven, our hopes to be renewed. O Eternal, Master of harmony, draw us close to You; resolve the discords of our lives. You in Whom all are one, lift us from the loneliness of self, and fill us with the fullness of Your love. Your greatness is beyond our praise. Raise us beyond the limits of our daily imperfections. Send us visions of the love that is in You, and of the good that may be in us.

Christian Readings & Prayers

New Testament Select Readings

The Lord's Prayer

Our Father who art in heaven,
  hallowed be Thy name.
Thy kingdom come, Thy will be done
  on earth as it is in heaven.
Give us this day our daily bread,
  and forgive us our trespasses
  as we forgive those who trespass against us;*
  and lead us not into temptation
  but deliver us from evil.
For thine is the kingdom, the power and the glory,
  now and forever. Amen.

*or "forgive us our debts as we forgive our debtors."

Matthew 6:25a, 26-27, 28b-30, 31a, 33-34 (NIV)

(Do not worry. Fear is one of the most common emotions one feels when in crisis. When praying for another it may be encouraging to include these words of Jesus.)

Therefore I tell you, do not worry about your life... Look at the birds of the air; they do not sow or reap or store away in barns, and yet your heavenly Father feeds them. Are you not much more valuable than they? Who of you by worrying can add a single hour to his life?

See how the lilies of the field grow. They do not labor or spin. Yet I tell you not even Solomon in all his splendor was dressed like one of these. If that is how God clothes the grass of the field...will he not much more clothe you, O you of little faith?

So do not worry... But seek first his kingdom and his righteousness, and all these things will be given to you as well. Therefore do not worry about tomorrow, for tomorrow will worry about itself. Each day has enough trouble of its own.

John 14:1-6 (NIV)
(In the Father's house are many dwellings.
A suitable passage following the death of a patient.)

"Do not let your hearts be troubled. Trust in God; trust also in me. In my Father's house there are many rooms; if it were not so, I would have told you. I am going there to prepare a place for you. And if I go and prepare a place for you, I will come back and take you to be with me that you also may be where I am. You know the way to the place where I am going." Thomas said to him, "Lord, we don't know where you are going, so how can we know the way?" Jesus answered, "I am the way and the truth and the life. No one comes to the Father except through me."

Jesus' Message on Forgiveness
(Matt 5:43-48, paraphrase by M. Sanders. Forgiveness of others and oneself helps bring healing to mind, emotions, body.)

People have told you, "Love your neighbor and hate your enemy." But I tell you this: Love your enemies and pray for those who disrespect you. Ask God to bless those who insult and hurt you. This is the way to truly live as the children of God.

God causes the sun to rise on those who do evil and those who do good, and sends life-giving rains for both the pure-of-heart and those who do violence.

If you love those who love you, are you doing anything special? No. Even unkind people do that. And if you show friendliness and kindness only to your family and small group of friends, is this unusual? Even those who do not realize that God exists do that much.

I want you to live at a higher level. Show great love by letting go of the desire to seek revenge; let go of the hatred you have in your heart. Be forgiving and gentle. Be understanding of the weaknesses and ignorance of others. Don't judge people harshly. You aren't wise enough to make a wise judgment about the condition of anyone's heart.

If you live this way, you will truly be living dignified lives as the children of God.

Acts 1:8a, 2:17a, 21 (NIV)
(The minister may offer a prayer that the patient will receive a greater experience of the Spirit in their lives; reading these quotes can help to root the prayer in Scripture.)

"But you will receive power when the Holy Spirit comes on you..." "I will pour out my Spirit on all people.

Your sons and daughters will prophesy, your young men will see visions, your old men will dream dreams." "And everyone who calls on the name of the Lord will be saved."

Galatians 5:16a, 22 (NIV)
(Fruit of the Spirit. The minister may offer this as a blessing, such as, "May you and your family be filled with the fruit of the Spirit...)

So I say, live by the Spirit... (T)he fruit of the Spirit is love, joy, peace, patience, kindness, goodness, faithfulness, gentleness and self-control.

Ephesians 3:14-21 (NIV)
(Prayer for spiritual power)

For this reason I kneel before the Father, from whom his whole family in heaven and on earth derives its name. I pray that out of his glorious riches he may strengthen you with power through his Spirit in your inner being, so that Christ may dwell in your hearts through faith. And I pray that you, being rooted and established in love, may have power, together with all the saints, to grasp how wide and long and high and deep is the love of Christ, and to know this love that surpasses knowledge—that you may be filled to the measure of all the fullness of God.

Now to him who is able to do immeasurably more than all we ask or imagine, according to his power that is at work within us, to him be glory in the church and in Christ Jesus throughout all generations, for ever and ever! Amen.

Philippians 4:4-9, 12a-13, 20 (NIV)
(Rejoice. Do not worry. Strength through God)

Rejoice in the Lord always. I will say it again: Rejoice! Let your gentleness be evident to all. The Lord is near. Do not be anxious about anything, but in everything, by prayer and petition, with thanksgiving, present your requests to God. And the peace of God, which transcends all understanding, will guard your hearts and your minds in Christ Jesus.

Finally, brothers [and sisters], whatever is true, whatever is noble, whatever is right, whatever is pure, whatever is lovely, whatever is admirable—if anything is excellent or praiseworthy—think about such things. Whatever you have learned or received or heard from me, or seen in me—put it into practice. And the God of peace will be with you.

I have learned the secret of being content in any and every situation, whether well fed or hungry, whether living in plenty or in want. I can do everything through him who gives me strength.

To our God and Father be glory forever. Amen.

Colossians 3:1-4, 10, 12-17 (NIV)
(Hope in Christ and God)

Since, then, you have been raised with Christ, set your hearts on things above, where Christ is seated at the right hand of God. Set your minds on things above, not on earthly things. For you died, and your life is now hidden with Christ in God. When Christ, who is your life, appears, then you also will appear with him in glory.

(P)ut on the new self, which is being renewed in knowledge in the image of its Creator.

Therefore, as God's chosen people, holy and dearly loved, clothe yourselves with compassion, kindness, humility, gentleness and patience. Bear with each other and forgive whatever grievances you may have against one another. Forgive as the Lord forgave you. And over all these virtues put on love, which binds them all together in perfect unity.

Let the peace of Christ rule in your hearts, since as members of one body you were called to peace. And be thankful. Let the word of Christ dwell in you richly as you teach and admonish one another with all wisdom, and as you sing psalms, hymns and spiritual songs with gratitude in your hearts to God. And whatever you do, whether in word or deed, do it all in the name of the Lord Jesus, giving thanks to God the Father through him.

James 1:2-6, 2:5, 4:7-8a (NIV)
(Encouragement when facing trials)

Consider it pure joy, my brothers [and sisters], whenever you face trials of many kinds, because you know that the testing of your faith develops perseverance. Perseverance must finish its work so that you may be mature and complete, not lacking anything. If any of you lacks wisdom, he should ask God, who gives generously to all without finding fault, and it will be given to him. But when he asks, he must believe and not doubt, because he who doubts is like a wave of the sea, blown and tossed by the wind.

Has not God chosen those who are poor in the eyes of the world to be rich in faith and to inherit the kingdom he promised those who love him?

Submit yourselves, then, to God. Resist the devil, and he will flee from you. Come near to God and he will come near to you.

James 5:13-18, 4:7a, 8a (NIV)
(Prayer for the sick with oil)

Is any of you in trouble? He should pray.

Is anyone happy? Let him sing songs of praise.

Is any one of you sick? He should call the elders of the church to pray over him and anoint him with oil in the name of the Lord. And the prayer offered in faith will make the sick person well*; the Lord will raise him up. If he has sinned, he will be forgiven. Therefore confess your sins to each other and pray for each other so that you may be healed. The prayer of a righteous man is powerful and effective.

Elijah was a man just like us. He prayed earnestly that it would not rain, and it did not rain on the land for three and a half years. Again he prayed, and the heavens gave rain, and the earth produced its crops.

Submit, yourselves, then, to God...Come near to God and he will come near to you.

*(*Note: There are different kinds of healing–healing of body, emotions, memory, morality, relationships, spiritual orientation; fear may be transformed into trust. The minister may find it appropriate to encourage the patient to be open to the multiple and unpredictable ways that healing may come.)*

— FROM THE CATHOLIC TRADITION —

The Deer's Cry / Breastplate of St. Patrick
(This is an edited version of the lengthy prayer, also known as The Lorica, dating back to the 5th Century Celtic tradition.)

I arise today through a mighty strength…
of the Creator of creation.
I arise today through the strength of heaven:
 light of sun, brilliance of moon,
 splendor of fire, speed of lightning,
 swiftness of wind, depth of sea,
 stability of earth, firmness of rock.
I arise today through God's strength
 to pilot me, God's strength to uphold me,
 God's wisdom to guide me…,
 God's ear to hear me…, God's hand to guard me,
 God's way to lie before me,
 God's shield to protect me,
 God's host to secure me.
Christ before me, Christ behind me.
 Christ above me, Christ below me.
 Christ on my left, Christ on my right. Amen.

Far Too Late Have I Begun to Love You
Augustine: Confessions X.27
(Translated by Henry Chadwick, modified by M. Sanders)

Far too late have I begun to love you,
Beauty so ancient and yet so new;
late have I loved you.

I now see You were within,
yet I was in the external world and sought you there,
and in my unlovely state
I plunged into those lovely things which you made.

You were with me, yet I was not with You.
The lovely things kept me far from You,
though if they did not have their existence in you
they would have had no existence at all.

You called and cried aloud and shattered my deafness.
You were radiant and resplendent;
You put to flight my blindness.
You were fragrant,
and I drew my breath and now pant after You.
I tasted You,
and I now feel such hunger and thirst for You.
You touched me,
and I am set on fire to attain the peace which is Yours.

All Shall be Well.

*Julian of Norwich (1342-1416), an English Christian mystic,
after having a vision in which she saw the hand of God holding
the entire world like a chestnut in His palm, was given this
beautiful affirmation of faith.)*

All shall be well,
 and all shall be well,
and all manner of thing
shall be well.

Let Nothing Disturb You
St. Teresa of Avila (1515-1582, Carmelite sister)

Let nothing disturb you.
 Let nothing frighten you.
All things are changing;
 God alone is changeless.
Patience attains the good.
One who has God lacks nothing.
 God alone fills all our needs.

Prayer of St. Francis

Lord, make me an instrument of your peace.
   Where there is hatred, let me sow love;
   where there is injury, pardon;
   where there is doubt, faith;
   where there is despair, hope;
   where there is darkness, light;
   where there is sadness, joy.
O Divine Master, grant that I may not so much seek to
be consoled as to console,
   not so much to be understood as to understand,
   not so much to be loved, as to love.
   For it is in giving that we receive,
   it is in pardoning that we are pardoned,
   and it is in dying that we awake to eternal life.

(The origin of this prayer is disputed. Franciscan scholars generally do not think it actually originated with Francis himself, but this does not diminish the spiritual and psychological wisdom contained herein.)

Prayer of St. Francis de Sales
(modified by Matt Sanders)

Do not look upon the changes and circumstances of this life in fear; rather, look upon them with full hope that as they arise God will deliver you out of them.

The one who has made you has kept you until now – so just hold fast to God's hand and you will be lead safely through all things. And when you cannot stand, God will bear you in His arms.

Do not look anxiously to what may happen tomorrow; the same everlasting God who cares for you today will also take care of you in all your tomorrows. Either you will be shielded from suffering or you will be given unfailing strength to bear it.

Be at peace, then, and put aside all anxious thoughts and imaginations.

You Are the Only Source of Health
(Adapted from The Catholic Devotional:
A Collection of Prayers and Inspiration for Every Catholic)

O God, you are the only ultimate Source of health and healing, the Spirit of calm in the storm,
 and the central Peace of the universe.

Grant this beloved one *(name)* a deeper awareness of Your indwelling presence and surrounding protection.

Calm *his/her* body and mind so *he/she* may be receptive to your gifts of healing and tranquility.

In whatever state *he/she* finds *himself / herself*, may *he/she* be a faithful servant of Thy love.

We pray in union with Christ Jesus the Great Physician. Amen.

How to Pray the Rosary
A. Structure:

1. Make the + *Sign of the Cross* and say the *Apostles Creed.*
2. Say the *Our Father.*
3. Say three *Hail Marys.*
4. Say the *Glory Be.*
5. Announce the First Mystery; then say the *Our Father.*
6. Say ten *Hail Marys* while meditating on the Mystery.
7. Say the *Glory Be*, then the *Fatima Prayer.*
8. Announce the Second Mystery; then say the *Our Father.* Repeat steps 6 & 7 and continue with the Third, Fourth and Fifth Mysteries in the same manner.
9. Say the *Hail Holy Queen.*
10. Conclude with the + *Sign of the Cross.*

B. Prayers:

+ Sign of the Cross: In the name of the Father and of the Son and of the Holy Spirit. Amen.

Apostles Creed: I believe in God, the Father Almighty, Creator of heaven and earth; and in Jesus Christ, His only Son, our Lord; who was conceived by the Holy Spirit, born of the Virgin Mary, suffered under Pontius Pilate, was crucified, died, and was buried. He descended into hell; the third day he rose again from the dead. He ascended into heaven, and is seated at the right hand of God, the Father Almighty; from thence he shall come to judge the living and the dead. I believe in the Holy Spirit, the holy Catholic Church, the communion of saints, the forgiveness of sins, the resurrection of the body, and life everlasting. Amen.

Our Father: Our Father who art in heaven, hallowed be Thy name. Thy kingdom come, Thy will be done on earth as it is in heaven. Give us this day our daily bread, and forgive us our trespasses as we forgive those who trespass against us; and lead us not into temptation but deliver us from evil. Amen.

Hail Mary: Hail Mary, full of grace, the Lord is with thee. Blessed art thou among women, and blessed is the fruit of thy womb, Jesus. Holy Mary, Mother of God, pray for us, sinners, now and at the hour of our death. Amen.

Glory Be: Glory be to the Father, and to the Son, and to the Holy Spirit, as it was in the beginning, is now and ever more shall be. Amen.

Fatima Prayer: O my Jesus, forgive us our sins, save us from the fires of hell, lead all souls to heaven, especially those who have most need of your mercy.

Hail, Holy Queen: Hail, Holy Queen, Mother of Mercy, our life, our sweetness and our hope, to you do we cry, poor banished children of Eve; to you do we send up our sighs, mourning and weeping in this vale of tears; turn then, most gracious Advocate, your eyes of mercy towards us, and after this, our exile, show unto us the blessed fruit of your womb, Jesus. O clement, O loving, O sweet Virgin Mary! Pray for us, O holy Mother of God, that we may be made worthy of the promises of Christ.

C. The Mysteries of the Rosary
(Suggested days to pray each mystery in parentheses):

Joyful Mysteries *(Monday & Saturday)*: Annunciation, Visitation, Birth of Jesus, Presentation, Finding of the Child Jesus in the Temple.

Luminous Mysteries/Mysteries of Light *(Thursday)*: Baptism of Jesus, Wedding at Cana, Proclamation of the Kingdom of God, Transfiguration, Institution of the Eucharist.

Sorrowful Mysteries *(Tuesday & Friday)*: Agony in the Garden, Scourging at the Pillar, Crowning with Thorns, Carrying of the Cross, Crucifixion.

Glorious Mysteries *(Wednesday & Sunday)*: Resurrection, Ascension, Descent of the Holy Spirit, Assumption of Mary, Coronation.

— FROM THE PROTESTANT TRADITION —

Serenity Prayer

(Reinhold Niebuhr, 1892-1971. The Serenity Prayer is one of the most popular prayers adopted by members of 12-Step groups such as Alcoholics Anonymous, Al-Anon, etc. Fewer people are familiar with the second half of the prayer written by Niebuhr, a Protestant theologian.)

God, grant me
    the **Serenity** to accept the things I cannot change;
    Courage to change the things I can;
    and the **Wisdom** to know the difference.

Living one day at a time,
    enjoying one moment at a time,
    accepting hardships as the pathway to peace;
    taking, as he did, this sinful world as it is, not as I would have it,
    trusting that He will make all things right if I surrender to His will;
    that I may be reasonably happy in this life
    and supremely happy with Him forever in the next.
Amen.

Prayer of an Unknown Soldier
(Source unknown)

I asked for strength that I might achieve; I was made weak that I might learn humbly to obey.

I asked for health that I might do greater things; I was given infirmity that I might do better things.

I asked for riches that I might be happy; I was given poverty that I might be wise.

I asked for power that I might have the praise of men; I was given weakness that I might feel the need of God.

I asked for all things that I might enjoy life; I was given life that I might enjoy all things.

I got nothing that I had asked for, but everything that I had hoped for. Almost despite myself my unspoken prayers were answered. I am, among all men, most richly blessed.

— FROM THE ORTHODOX TRADITION —

Pilgrim Prayer
(From The Way of a Pilgrim, an Eastern Orthodox classic, by an anonymous narrator, mid-nineteenth century Russia.)

Lord Jesus Christ, have mercy on me.

(A shortened version of this prayer is to simply say the name of Jesus with another word that has meaning for the individual, such as:)

Jesus, mercy.
Jesus, heal me.
Jesus, love.

Behold!
(From the Byzantine Orthodox liturgy.)

Behold!
Today is the day of the Resurrection.
Let us glory in the feast.
Let us embrace one another in joy and say:
   O friends and enemies too,
   we forgive everything
   on Resurrection Day!

"Jesus Christ Conquers All!"
(This prayer is suitable when battling against evil of any kind including evil that comes from the world, the flesh, or the devil.)

Baha'i Prayers

O God! Refresh and Gladden my Spirit
'Abdu'l-Baha

O God! Refresh and gladden my spirit. Purify my heart. Illumine my powers. I lay all my affairs in Thy hand. Thou art my Guide and my Refuge. I will no longer be sorrowful and grieved; I will be a happy and joyful being.

O God! I will no longer be full of anxiety, nor will I let trouble harass me. I will not dwell on the unpleasant things of life.

O God! Thou art more friend to me than I am to myself. I dedicate myself to Thee, O Lord.

(From "'Abdu'l-Baha, Baha'i Prayers: A Selection of Prayers Revealed by Baha'u'llah, the Bab, and 'Abdu'l-Baha." Wilmette: Baha'i Publishing Trust, 1982, p. 152. Used with permission. 'Abdu'l-Baha (d. 1921) was the eldest son of Baha'u'llah, the prophet-founder of the Baha'i faith.)

Strive

Strive that your actions day-by-day may be beautiful prayers. Turn towards God and seek always to do that which is right and noble: enrich the poor, raise the fallen, comfort the sorrowful, bring healing to the sick, reassure the fearful, rescue the oppressed, bring hope to the hopeless, shelter the destitute! Strive!

(These are song lyrics based on a talk given in 1911 by Abdu'l- Baha, Baha'u'llah's eldest son and appointed successor. Source: http://www. youtube.com/watch?v=4y2WGjl_9n 4&feature=related. Musical setting Joe Crone.)

The following six quotes are taken from The Baha'i Faith: An Introduction, *Gloria Faizi, Baha'i Publishing Trust, New Delhi, India, 1992. Page numbers are cited.*

Create in Me a Pure Heart
Baha'u'llah

Create in me a pure heart, O my God, and renew a tranquil conscience within me, O my Hope! Through the spirit of power confirm Thou me in Thy Cause, O my Best-Beloved, and by the light of Thy glory reveal unto me thy path, O Thou the Goal of my desire! Through the power of Thy transcendent might lift me up unto the heaven of Thy holiness, O Source of my being, and by the breezes of Thine eternity gladden me, O Thou Who art my God! Let Thine everlasting melodies breathe tranquility on me, O my Companion, and let the riches of Thine ancient countenance deliver me from all except Thee, O my Master, and let the tidings of the revelation of Thine incorruptible Essence bring me joy, O thou Who art the most manifest of the manifest and the most hidden of the hidden! (p.56-7)

Words of Encouragement and Inspiration
Baha'u'llah

O Son of Spirit! My first counsel is this: Possess a pure, kindly and radiant heart, that thine may be a sovereignty ancient, imperishable and everlasting.

O Son of Man! Be thou content with me and seek no other helper. For none but Me can ever suffice thee.

O Son of Spirit! With the joyful tidings of light I hail thee: rejoice! To the court of holiness I summon thee; abide therein that thou mayest live in peace for evermore.

O Son of Being! Thy heart is My home; sanctify it for My descent. Thy spirit is My place of revelation; cleanse it for My manifestation.

(Faizi attributes this to the Hidden Words of Baha'u'llah [God's Eternal Call to Man], p.73-4)

Thy Name is My Healing
Baha'u'llah

Thy Name is my healing, o my God, and remembrance of Thee is my remedy, nearness to thee is my hope, and love for Thee is my companion. Thy mercy to me is my healing and my succor in both this world and the world to come.

(succor: assistance when in distress)

Unite the Hearts of Thy Servants
Baha'u'llah

O my God! O my God! Unite the heart of thy servants, and reveal to them thy great purpose. May they follow thy commandments and abide in thy law. Help them, o God, in their endeavor, and grant them strength to serve thee, o God! Leave them not to themselves, but guide their steps by the light of thy knowledge, and cheer their hearts by thy love. Verily, thou art their helper and their Lord.

Sorrow and Promise of Heavenly Delight
Baha'u'llah

Sorrow not if, in these days and on this earthly plane, things contrary to your wishes have been ordained and manifested by God, for days of blissful joy, of heavenly delight, are assuredly in store for you. Worlds, holy and spiritually glorious, will be unveiled to your eyes. You are destined by Him, in this world and hereafter, to partake of their benefits, to share in their joys, and to obtain a portion of their sustaining grace. To each and every one of them you will, no doubt, attain. (p. 58-9)

Death and Grieving
Baha'u'llah

O Son of the Supreme! I have made death a messenger of joy to thee. Wherefore dost thou grieve? I made the light to shed on thee its splendor. Why dost thou veil thyself therefrom? (p. 62)

Buddhist Prayers

The Only Moment
Thich Nhat Hanh

Breathing in, I calm body and mind.
Breathing out, I smile with joy.
Dwelling in the present, this is the only moment.

(Thich Nhat Hanh is a Vietnamese Buddhist monk known worldwide for his peace activism.)

One Breath
Thich Nhat Hanh

One breath to let go.
One breath to be present.
One breath to ask, "Now what?"

The Prajnaparamita Heart Sutra

Gate, gate,
paragate,
parasamgate,
Bohhi, svaha!

Translation: Gone, gone, gone all the way over,
everyone gone to the other shore,
enlightenment, *svaha*!

("Svaha is a cry of joy or excitement like 'Welcome!' or 'Hallelujah!'" Source: Thich Nhat Hanh, The Heart of Understanding: Commentaries on the Prajnaparamita Heart Sutra, Parallax Press, Berkeley, 1988. p. 50)

Mindfulness of Beloved Ones
Thich Nhat Hanh

Brothers and sisters, it is time to bring our beloved ones to mind; those to whom we wish to send the healing energy of love and compassion. Let us sit and enjoy our breathing for a few moments, allowing our beloved ones to be present with us now.
[Ten breaths in silence.]

Protecting and Transforming
Thich Nhat Hanh

We, your disciples, from beginningless time, have made ourselves unhappy out of confusion and ignorance, being born and dying with no direction, have now found confidence in the highest awakening.

However much we may have drifted on the ocean of suffering, today we see clearly that there is a beautiful path. We turn toward the light of loving-kindness to direct us. We bow deeply to the Awakened One and to our spiritual ancestors, who light up the path before us, guiding every step. *[bell]*

The wrongdoings and sufferings that imprison us are brought about by craving, hatred, ignorance and pride. Today, we begin anew to purify and free our hearts. With awakened wisdom, bright as the sun and the full moon, and immeasurable compassion to help humankind, we resolve to live beautifully. With all of our heart we go for refuge to the Three Precious Jewels.

With the boat of loving-kindness we cross over the ocean of suffering. With the light of wisdom we leave behind the forest of confusion. With determination, we learn, reflect and practice. Right view is the ground of our actions in body, speech and mind.

Right mindfulness embraces us, walking, standing, lying down, and sitting, speaking, smiling, coming in and going out. Whenever anger or anxiety enter our heart, we are determined to breathe mindfully and come back to ourselves. With every step we will walk within the Pure Land. With every look the Dharmakaya is revealed. We are careful and attentive as sense organs touch sense objects so all habit energies can be observed and easily transformed.

May our heart's garden of awakening bloom with hundreds of flowers. May we bring the feelings of peace and joy into every household. May we plant wholesome seeds on the ten thousand paths. May we never have the need to leave the Sangha body. May we never attempt to leave the sufferings of the world, always being present whenever beings need our help. May mountains and rivers be our witness in this moment as we bow our heads and request the Lord of Compassion to embrace us all. *[two bells]*

(Source of previous two passages: Thich Nhat Hanh, Plum Village Chanting and Recitation Book, Berkeley, CA, Parallax Press, 2000, as quoted in Prayers & Rituals at a Time of Illness and Dying, Pat Fosarelli, Templeton Foundation Press, 2008, p.11-13)

A Zen Poem
P'ang-Yun

How wonderful!
Quite miraculous!
I am fetching water,
and carrying wood!

(This 8th Century Chinese Zen master has expressed the wonder and joy found in the here-and-now of life.)

The Bodhisattva Vow:

May I attain Buddhahood
for the benefit of all sentient beings.

(The Bodhisattva Vow is essential to Mahayana and Tibetan Buddhism. Various forms are in use.)

Three Treasures

I take refuge in Buddha. May we all together absorb into ourselves the principle of Your Way Enlightenment and awaken in ourselves our Supreme Will.

I take refuge in Dharma. May we all together be submerged in the depth of Thy Doctrine and get wisdom as deep as the ocean.

I take refuge in Sangha. May we all together become units in true accord in Your Life of Harmony in a spirit of Universal Brotherhood, freed from the bondage of selfishness.

Three Chants:

(The following chants come from three different Buddhist traditions. Volumes have been written about the meaning of these chants, thus there are no English translations which can simply and adequately capture their meanings Interested persons are encouraged to study their meanings more deeply.)

Om Mani Padme Hum

From the Tibetan tradition. Suggested translations: "The jewel is in the lotus." "Praise to be the jewel in the lotus." "Jewel-Lotus!" *"This is the Mantra of Avalokitesvara (Chenresig), otherwise known as the Six-Syllable Mantra of Great Compassion. Volumes have been written on the meaning of this mantra, but simply, it invokes the greatest compassionate prayers for the elimination of suffering on all realms of existence, the purification of all negative karmas, and the ripening of all spiritual attainments." - Rev. Susan Shannon*

Namu Amida Butsu

From the Japanese Pure Land tradition. Suggested translations: "Hail to Amitābha Buddha" *(source: answers.com)*. "Total reliance upon the compassion of Amida Buddha" *(source: http://blog. livingspark.net/2008/11/buddhist-chant-namu-amida-butsu.html)* Shinran writes: *"It is taught, concerning Namu-amida-butsu, That its virtue is like the vast waters of the ocean; Having myself received that pure good, I direct it equally to all sentient beings." (Source: The Collected Works of Shinran, Vol. I, Jodo Shinshu Hongwanji-ha Horikawa-dori, Shimogyo-ku, Kyoto Japan, 1997, p. 393.)*

Nam Myoho Renge Kyo

This Nichiren [Japanese] Buddhist chant is based on the *Lotus Sutra*. Suggested translations: "I devote myself to the mystic law of cause and effect through sound." "I take refuge in (devote or submit myself to) The Wonderful Law of the Lotus Flower Sutra" *(source: http://en.wikipedia.org/wiki/Daimoku)*.

Parable of Kisa Gotami and the Poppyseed

Once there was a young woman named Kisagotami, the wife of a wealthy man, who lost her mind because of the death of her child. She took the dead child in her arms and went from house to house begging people to heal the child.

Of course, they could do nothing for her, but finally a follower of Buddha advised her to see the Blessed One who was then staying at Jetavana, and so she carried the dead child to Buddha.

The Blessed One looked upon her with sympathy and said: "To heal the child I need some poppy seeds; go and beg four or five poppy seeds from some home where death has never entered."

So the demented woman went out and sought a house where death had never entered, but in vain. At last, she was obliged to return to Buddha. In his quiet presence her mind cleared and she understood the meaning of his words. She took the body away and buried it, and then returned to Buddha and became one of his disciples.

(Source: The Teaching of Buddha, Bukkyo Dendo Kyokai, Society for the Promotion of Buddhism, Tokyo, 1966, pp. 94-5.) In a talk to chaplains in Citrus Heights, CA, Japanese Pure Land Buddhist Minister Rev. Bob Oshita indicated this is one of the most important parables of Buddhism that a chaplain may want to utilize in a pastoral setting.

In one variation of this parable the Buddha instructs Kisa Gotami to search for some mustard seed rather than poppyseed but the lessons remain the same. Edwin A. Burtt, in The Teachings of the Compassionate Buddha, *comments: "Two of Buddha's most important doctrines are taught [in this parable]...: [1] Everything in the realm of phenomenal existence is in change and is transitory...Hence a realistic acceptance of death is an essential part of true adjustment to reality. [2] This story reveals the essential connection...between a realistic acceptance of death and the realization of an outgoing compassion toward all living beings who, like ourselves, are subject to such ills."* (The Teachings of the Compassionate Buddha, *Mentor Books, 1982, p. 43).*

Hindu Prayers

Vedic Prayer: Thou Art the Protector
(M. B. Shah. Bhavi Intl., Bombay, India.)

O! All powerful God, Thou art the protector of the whole physical creation; may Thou protect my body.

Thou art the source of all life. Thou art the source of all strength; may Thou make me strong.

O, omnipotent Lord, I look to thee to fill up all my wants and to give me healing: physical, mental and spiritual.

Hindu Prayer for Peace

Oh God, lead us from the unreal to the Real. Oh God, lead us from darkness to light. Oh God, lead us from death to immortality.

*Shanti, Shanti, Shanti** unto all.

Oh Lord God almighty, may there be peace in celestial regions. May there be peace on earth. May the waters be appeasing. May herbs be wholesome, and may trees and plants bring peace to all.

May all beneficent beings bring peace to us. May thy Vedic Law propagate peace all through the world. May all things be a source of peace to us. And may thy peace itself bestow peace on all, and may that peace come to me also.

(*Shanti is Sanskrit for peace. This prayer is part of the 12-prayer series gathered in Assisi, Italy on the day of prayer for world peace during the United Nations International Year for Peace, 1986. The prayers were entrusted to the care of Life Experience School and Peace Abbey, Massachusetts.)

OM or AUM

This is the primordial sound, the holy syllable, the vibratory aspect of Brahman. The Katha Upanishad indicates: "Those in whose hearts OM reverberates unceasingly are indeed blessed."

From the Bhagavad Gita

Author Pat Fosarelli writes: "Reading particularly apropos verses of the Bhagavad Gita can ...be comforting (to the ill or dying). The following verses...are attributed to Lord Krishna (God), as he spoke gently to the warrior, Arjuna, who was sorrowful over having to kill in battle. His words underscore the impermanence of death and the importance of devotion to God." (Source: Prayers & Rituals at a Time of Illness & Dying: The Practices of Five World Religions, Pat Fosarelli, Templeton Foundation Press, 2008, pp. 50-51). Except where indicated the quotes below are from Bhagavad-Gita As It Is, A.C. Bhaktivedanta Swami Prabhupada.

Three quotes on the impermanence of death:

The Soul Accepts New Bodies
(Bhagavad Gita 2:22)

As a person puts on new garments, giving up old ones, similarly, the soul accepts new material bodies, giving up the old and useless ones.

The Soul is Immutable; Grieve Not the Body
(Bhagavad Gita 2:24-28)

This individual soul is unbreakable and insoluble and can be neither burned nor dried. He is everlasting, all-pervading, unchangeable, immovable and eternally the same. It is said that the soul is invisible, inconceivable, immutable and unchangeable. Knowing this, you should not grieve for the body.

If, however, you think the soul is perpetually born and always dies, still you have no reason to lament, O mighty-armed. For one who has taken his birth, death is certain; and for one who is dead, birth is certain. Therefore, in the unavoidable discharge of your duty, you should not lament.

All created beings are unmanifest in their beginning, manifest in their interim state, and unmanifest again when they are annihilated. So what need is there for lamentation?"

The Wise Lament Not;
The Soul Passes to Another Body at Death
(Bhagavad Gita 2:11b-13)

Those who are wise lament neither for the living nor the dead.

Never was there a time when I did not exist, nor you, nor all these kings; nor in the future shall any of us cease to be.

As the embodied soul continually passes, in this body, from boyhood to youth, and then to old age, the soul similarly passes into another body at death. The self-realized soul is not bewildered by such a change.

Additional quotes on the Impermanence of Death:

2:16-17 No one can destroy the imperishable soul.

2:20   For the soul there is neither birth nor death.

Four quotes on the importance of devotion to God:

Detached Action, Unattachment to Results
(Bhagavad Gita 2:47)

Set thy heart upon thy work, but never on its reward. Work not for a reward; but never cease to do thy work. Do thy work in the peace of Yoga and, free from selfish desires, be not moved in success or in failure. Yoga is evenness of mind—a peace that is ever the same. *(Source: Fosarelli, p. 52, translated by Mascaro)*

Free from Ego One Attains Real Peace
(Bhagavad Gita 2:70-72)

A person who is not disturbed by the incessant flow of desires—that enter like rivers into the ocean, which is ever being filled but is always still—can alone achieve peace, and not the man who strives to satisfy such desires.

A person who has given up all desires for sense gratification, who lives free from desires, who has given up all sense of proprietorship and is devoid of false ego—he alone can attain real peace.

That is the way of the spiritual and godly life, after attaining which a man is not bewildered. Being so situated, even at the hour of death, one can enter into the kingdom of God.

Remember God at the Moment of Death
(Bhagavad Gita 8:2b, 3a, 5)

[Arjuna inquired:] And how can those engaged in devotional service know You at the time of death?

[Krishna] The Supreme Personality of Godhead replied: The indestructible, transcendental living entity is called Brahman...

Anyone who, at the end of life, quits his body remembering Me, attains immediately to My nature, and there is no doubt of this.

Always Think of Me;
Be Freed from the Misery of Rebirth
(Bhagavad Gita 8:7, 15-16,
translation to English by Mikhail Nikolenko)

Therefore, remember Me always — and fight. Aspiring to Me with the mind and consciousness, you will surely enter Me!

Having come to Me, such Mahatmas never get born again in this transient vale of tears: they attain the Highest Perfection.

Those dwelling in the worlds lower than the world of Brahman get born again, O Arjuna! But they who have attained Me are not subject to new births!

(Source of the following: Interfaith Resources Book of Comfort & Healing, 2010. InterfaithResources.com)

You Become Still
(Peace through acceptance of reality as it is.)
(Ashtavakra Gita 11:1)

All things arise, Suffer change, and pass away.
This is their nature. When you know this,
Nothing perturbs you, nothing hurts you.
You become still. It is easy.

May No One Suffer Pain
(The Hindu Prayer Book)

O Lord in Thee may all be happy.
May all be free from misery.
May all realize goodness and may no one suffer pain.

Fly to Me Alone!
(Bhagavad Gita, Edwin Arnold tr.)

Fly to Me alone! Make Me thy single refuge!
I will free Thy soul from all its sins!
Be of good cheer!

Prayers from Islam

"La ilaha illa Allah wa Muhammad ar-rasulullah."

"There is no god, but Allah, and Muhammad is the messenger of Allah."

Note: In my pastoral experience, Muslim believers respectfully follow their own prayer discipline rather than request additional prayerful support from a non-Muslim chaplain. Daily prayers, five times daily, are recited in Arabic accompanied with standing, kneeling, and prostration; these are prescribed, and not extemporaneous prayers. It has been my experience that the chaplain's role is to help advocate for the Muslim patient/prisoner who wishes to have uninterrupted time for prayer.

Oh Allah
(A du'a [prayer of supplication] of Muhammad, pbuh)

Oh Allah! I am your servant, son of Your servant, son of Your maidservant; my forehead is in Your Hand; Your judgment is exact; Your decision about me is just.

I ask You by every name of Yours which You have called Yourself, or revealed in a Book of Yours, or taught to any of Your servants, or reserved within Your unrevealed Knowledge, to make the Qur'an a spring to my heart, a light in my chest, that it remove my sadness, and erase my anguish.

(The following two quotes from the Qur'an come from The Meanings of The Illustrious Qur'an without Arabic text, by Abdullah Yusuf Ali)

Surah 1:1-7
Al-Fatiha (The Opening)

In the name of Allah, Most Gracious, Most Merciful. Praise be to Allah, the Cherisher and Sustainer of the worlds; Most Gracious, Most Merciful; Master of the Day of Judgment. You (alone) do we worship, and Your aid we seek. Show us the straight way, The way of those on whom You has (sic) bestowed Your Grace, those whose (portion) is not wrath, and who go not astray.

Surah 24:35
Al-Noor Or (The Light)

Allah is the Light of the heavens and the Earth. The parable of His Light is as if there were a niche and within it a lamp, the lamp enclosed in glass, the glass as it were a brilliant star, lit from a blessed tree, an olive, neither of the east nor of the west. Whose oil is well luminous, though Fire scarce touched it, light upon light! Allah does guide whom He will to His Light: Allah does set forth parables for me, and Allah does know all things.

Call to Prayer
*(English translation which the muezzin
calls Muslims to prayer five times a day:)*

God is most great. God is most great.
God is most great. God is most great.
I testify that there is no god except God.
I testify that there is no god except God.
I testify that Muhammad is the messenger of God.
I testify that Muhammad is the messenger of God.
Come to prayer! Come to prayer!
Come to success (in this life and the Hereafter)!
Come to success!
God is most great. God is most great.
There is no god except God.

The Guesthouse
Rumi (1207-1273)

This being human is a guest-house, every morning a new arrival: a joy, a depression, a meanness, some momentary awareness comes as an unexpected visitor.

Welcome and entertain them all, even if they're a crowd of sorrows who violently sweep your house empty of its furniture.

Still, treat each guest honorably. He may be clearing you out for some new delight.

The dark thought, the shame, the malice, meet them at the door laughing, and invite them in.

Be grateful for whoever comes, because each has been sent as a guide from beyond.

Native American Prayers

In a Sacred Manner
Eagleboy

Creator of all that exists, hear my prayer.

As the new day dawns let all people begin anew to walk the good road of life. May we forget our differences, may we remember our likenesses. Let us hear what we have not heard; let us see what we have not seen. You are the Spark of the universe, the Oneness of all life.

In such a way may we be blessed, blessed in a sacred manner.

Sioux Chief's Prayer

Oh Great Spirit, Whose voice I hear in the winds, and whose breath gives life to all the world, hear me! I come before You, one of your many children. I am small and weak; I need your strength and wisdom. Let me walk in beauty and make my eyes ever behold the red and purple sunset. Make my hands respect the things you have made, my ears sharp to hear your voice. Make me wise so that I may know the things you have taught my people, the lessons you have hidden in every leaf and rock. I seek not to be superior to my brothers, but to be able to fight my greatest enemy—myself. Make me ever ready to come to you with clean hands and straight eyes, so when life fades, as a fading sunset, my spirit may come to you without shame.

Sikh Prayers

Keep Me, O Lord
Guru Granth Sahib (Sikh Scripture)

I pray before Thee. The soul and body are Thine. All
are Thine and Thou art for all... Thou art the Lord and
I offer my prayer to Thee. The soul and body are Thy
commodities. Thou art the Mother and Father and we
are Thy children. Keep me, O Lord, under Thy shelter,
by Thy grace.

Night and day, meditate in remembrance on the One
who will be your Help and Support in the end. *(Guru
Granth Sahib, section 7)*

Sing the glories of God each and every day; your
afflictions shall be dispelled, and you shall be saved, my
humble friend. *(Guru Granth Sahib, section 7)*

Those humble beings who struggle with their minds
are brave and distinguished heroes. Those who realize
their own selves, remain forever united with the Lord.
This is the glory of the spiritual teachers, that they remain

absorbed in their mind. They attain the Mansion of the Lord's Presence, and focus their meditation on the True Lord. Those who conquer their own minds...conquer the world. *(Guru Granth Sahib, section 25)*

The Love of the Lord is the healing remedy; the Name of the Lord is the healing remedy. *(Guru Granth Sahib, section 27)*

O mind, there is only the One medicine, mantra and healing herb—center your consciousness firmly on the One Lord. *(Guru Granth Sahib, section 7)*

Unity-Style Prayers

Prayer for Protection

The light of God surrounds me;
The love of God enfolds me;
The power of God protects me;
The presence of God watches over me.
Where I am, God is!
And all is well!

God is My Help

Hanna More Kohaus

God is my help in every need,
   God does my every hunger feed,
Walks beside me, guides my way,
 Through every moment of the day.
I now am wise, I now am true,
   Patient, kind and loving too.
All things I am, can do and be
   Through God, the Truth that is in me.
God is my health, I cannot be sick,
   God is my strength, unfailing and quick.

God is my all, I know no fear,
Since God and Love and Truth are here.

I Breathe

Matt Sanders.
(Breathe consciously at the end of each "I breathe".)

I breathe...

With this breath I breathe in all the goodness of God; this goodness is my inheritance. I remember my identity: I am a child of God, precious and free.

I breathe in unconditional love...

I express unconditional love for myself. I express compassion for others who come to mind. I let go of all hurts and negativity and forgive everything on this day! I imagine the unconditional love of God radiating through me, from my heart, radiating to myself and all those who come to mind.

I breathe in healing...

Healing comes to me in many ways: healing of body, emotions, memories, thoughts, relationships. This moment is filled with grace and gentleness; healing is happening even now!

I breathe in courage...

As I face the struggles of life I exercise the inner muscle of courage. I continue to wrestle with the struggles that come my way, trusting that I am being strengthened in soul.

I breathe...

This breath is my prayer of trust. Amen.

From the 12-Step Tradition

I Can't
(A prayer summary of Steps 1, 2 & 3)

I can't.
God can.
I think I'll let Him.

Thank You for...

God, Thank you for what you've given me.
Thank you for what you've taken away.
Thank you for what you've left.

*This prayer calls to mind the slogan "attitude of gratitude" and
is illustrated in this poem as quoted by Dale Carnegie in "How
To Stop Worrying and Start Living":*
> *I had the blues
> 'cause I had no shoes,
> Til on the street
> I met a man who had no feet.*

Third Step Prayer
(Alcoholics Anonymous Big Book, p. 63)

God, I offer myself to Thee, to build with me and to do with me as Thou wilt. Relieve me of the bondage of self, that I may better do Thy will. Take away my difficulties, that victory over them may bear witness to those I would help of Thy power, Thy love and Thy way of life. May I do Thy will always.

Fourth Step Reflection
(Alcoholics Anonymous Big Book, p. 67)

"This is a sick man. How can I be helpful to him? God save me from being angry. Thy will be done."

Seventh Step Prayer
(Alcoholics Anonymous Big Book, p. 76)

My Creator, I am now willing that You should have all of me, good and bad. I pray that You now remove from me every single defect of character which stands in the way of my usefulness to You and my fellows. Grant me strength as I go out from here, to do Your bidding. Amen.

Tenth Step Prayer
(Alcoholics Anonymous Big Book, p. 85)

How can I best serve Thee?
Thy will (not mine) be done.

Pettiness Prayer
(From AA prayer pamphlet)

Keep us, oh God, from pettiness. Let us be large in thought, in word, in deed. Let us be through with faultfinding and leave off self-seeking. May we put away all pretense and meet each other face to face, without self-pity or without prejudice. May we always be patient, never hasty in judgment and always tolerant. Teach us to put into action our better impulses, straightforward and unafraid. Let us take time for all things; make us calm, serene and gentle. Grant that we may realize that it is the little things in life that make the differences, that in the big things we are as one. And may we strive to touch and to know the great common heart of us all. And oh God, let us not forget to be kind.

Misc. Prayers

Short Affirmative Prayers

The most useful prayers are often the simplest. Below are one-word prayers and short phrases which are helpful when used throughout one's day or during contemplative prayer. The chaplain may find it appropriate to suggest one or more of these prayers to a patient.

- "Yes."
- "Help."
- "I trust."
- "I believe."
- "I'm sorry."
- "Thank You."
- "I praise You."
- "All shall be well."
- "Thy will be done."
- "Let go and let God."
- "This, too, shall pass."
- "Your joy is my strength."
- "In Your will is my peace."

- "I return to the Good Path."
- "You make all things work together for good."
- breathe

I Don't Like It
Matt Sanders

I don't like it,
but I accept it.
Thank you God.

Celtic Blessing

May the roads rise to meet you,
May the wind be always at your back,
May the sun shine warm upon your face,
The rain fall soft upon your fields
And, until we meet again,
May God hold you in the hollow of his hand.

PART 2

PRAYERS IN FOREIGN LANGUAGES

Russian

Ti ne pechalsya
 ne bespa koysya
yesli boch snami
 chevo bayatsa

Translation: Don't worry, don't be sad,
since God is for us, what is there to fear?

Spanish: Sign of the Cross

En el nombre del Padre
Del Hijo
Y del Espíritu Santo. Amén.

Spanish: Padre Nuestro (Our Father)

Padre nuestro, que estás en el cielo,
Santificado sea Tu nombre;
venga a nosotros tu Reino;
hágase tu voluntad
en la tierra como en el cielo.
Danos hoy nuestro pan de cada día,
y perdona nuestras ofensas,
como también nosotros perdonamos
a los que nos ofenden;
no nos dejes caér en las tentación,
y líbranos de todo mal. Amén.

Spanish: Ave Maria (Hail Mary)

Dios te salve, María, llena eres de gracia, el Señor es contigo; bendita tú eres entre todas las mujeres, y bendito es el fruto de tu vientre, Jesús. Santa María, Madre de Dios, ruega por nosotros pecadores, ahora y en la hora de nuestra muerte. Amén.

Spanish: Goria (Glory)

Gloria al Padre, y al Hijo, y al Espéritu Santo. Como era en el principio, ahora y siempre por los siglos de los siglos. Amén.

Spanish: Psalm 46:10

Be still and know that I am God.
Estad tranquilos y conoced que yo soy Dios.

Spanish: Psalm 23:1

The Lord is my shepherd, there is nothing I shall want.
El Señor es mi pastor, nada me falta.

Spanish: Prayer/Song for Contemplation

Slowly blooms the rose within.
Que la rosa dentro de si, florezca lentamente.

Tagalog (Filipino): Ama Namin (Our Father)

Ama namin sumasalangit ka,
Sambahin ang ngalan mo;
Mapasa-amin ang kaharian mo,
Sundin ang loob mo
Dito sa lupa para nang sa langit.

Bigyan mo kami ngayon
Ng aming kakanin sa araw-araw;
At patawarin mo kami sa aming mga sala
Para nang pagpapatawad namin
Sa mga nagkakasala sa amin,
At huwag mo kaming
ipahintulot sa tukso
At iadya mo kami
sa lahat ng masama.

PART 3

PRAYERS FOR SPECIFIC CIRCUMSTANCES IN A HOSPITAL SETTING

Note: For a chaplain working in an interfaith capacity it is important to consider the faith traditions of one's patients/ clients. The following question may be helpful to incorporate into one's ministerial approach: "It's important to us (e.g. hospital staff) that we honor the faith traditions of all our patients. Do you have a faith tradition that is important to you?"

Many of the following prayers include traditional names and images for God. You may want to ask a patient: "Is there a name or image of God that is especially meaningful to you?"

Communion at the bedside

A. Minimal Form:
+ The Body of Christ.
R: **Amen.**

B. Brief Form:
(Eucharistic Minister. **Response**.)

1. *Invite the communicant to take a moment to calm body and mind.*

2. *+ Make the Sign of the Cross.*

3. Lord, you heal the contrite.
   Lord have mercy.
   Lord have mercy.

   Christ, you comfort the weak.
   Christ have mercy.
   Christ have mercy.

   Lord,you are the Divine Physician.
   Lord have Mercy.
   Lord have mercy.

4. *A brief quote or sentence from Scripture may be spoken.* *

5. We lift up our prayer intentions. *(May speak intentions.)*

6. **Our Father...**

7. *Holding up the consecrated host:*

Behold the Lamb of God;
behold Him who takes away the sins of the world,
blessed are those called to the supper of the Lamb.

R: **Lord, I am not worthy that you should enter under my roof, but only say the word and my soul shall be healed.**

8. + The body of Christ. **R: Amen**.

9. *Invite the communicant to take a moment of silence and gratitude to mindfully commune with the Lord.*

10. *Closing: Song or Brief Prayer such as:*
Glory & Praise to Our God (Dan Schutte, S.J.)

or: Psalm 118:29: Give thanks to the Lord for he is good; his love is everlasting.

Readings:
- Ps 23:1-6 (The Lord is my Shepherd, p. 11)
- Jn 14:1-6 (Do not let your hearts be troubled, p. 26)
- Mt 11:28 (Come to me all who are weary and heaven burdened and I will give you rest.)
- Mt 9:20-22 (healing of sick woman, touch cloak)
- Mk 15:34ff (Good Friday)
- Lk 24: 30-32 (Emmaus)

Baptism

The basic and essential elements for baptism are provided below. These can be supplemented with appropriate Scripture readings and/or songs. The Roman Catholic tradition maintains that in the event of an emergency anyone can baptize a non-baptized person. Surprisingly, even a person not of the Christian faith can baptize another, if that person so desires.

Baptismal Formula

1. Pour a few drops of water on the forehead, or trace the Sign of the Cross. .

2. Recite the Baptismal Formula as given by Jesus in the New Testament:
   "I baptize you in the name of the Father, and of the Son, and of the Holy Spirit. Amen."

Provide for the newly baptized person a certificate stating: "(Name) has been baptized in the in the name of the Father, and of the Son, and of the Holy Spirit." Notate date, location, minister. Keep appropriate records.

Baptism, Lengthier Format

+ (Sign of the Cross) We gather at this moment for the sacrament of baptism.

Song: (Such as *Glory & Praise to our God* by Dan Schutte)

A reading from Paul's letter to the Romans 6:3-4.
> Did you forget that all of us became part of Christ when we were baptized? We shared his death in our baptism. When we were baptized, we were buried with Christ and shared his death. So, just as Christ was raised from the dead by the wonderful power of the Father, we also can live a new life. (*New Century Version*)

A reading from the Gospel of Matthew 28:18-20
Following the Resurrection of Christ Jesus:
> Jesus drew near and said to them, "I have been given all authority in heaven and on earth. Go, then, to all peoples everywhere and make them my disciples: baptize them in the name of the Father, the Son, and the Holy Spirit, and teach them to obey everything I have commanded you. And I will be with you always, to the end of the age." (*Good News Translation*)

Do you turn away from sin, and the devil, and all his empty promises? *Response:* I do.

Do you seek to love God, do God's will, and follow Christ Jesus?   *Response:* I do.

Do you wish to receive baptism thus be more deeply united with God through Christ in the power of the Holy Spirit?   *Response:* I do.

Our Father who art in heaven, hallowed be Thy name. Thy kingdom come, Thy will be done on earth as it is in heaven. Give us this day our daily bread, and forgive us our trespasses as we forgive those who trespass against us; and lead us not into temptation but deliver us from evil.

[For thine is the kingdom, the power and the glory, now and forever. Amen.]

(Baptismal Formula)
Name: _____, I baptize you in the name of the Father, and of the Son, and of the Holy Spirit. Amen.

Song: You have been baptized in Christ.
        It is he that you have put on.
        You who are washed in this water
        have hope for eternal life.

Prayer: Gracious and loving God, we thank you that by water and the Holy Spirit you have bestowed upon this *son/daughter* the forgiveness of sin and have raised *him/her* in newness of life of grace. Bless *him/her*, O Lord, with an increase in thy Spirit, enfold *him/her* in your arms of mercy, keeping *him/her* safe forever. Amen.

Blessing for Healthy Newborn

Baby: _____
Mother: _____
Father: _____

Optional Introduction

1. What name do you give your child?

2. Editor's comment: My own mother gave each of her nine children back to God, saying, "This is not my child, Lord, I give him to You."

3. This baby has already been blessed with life and love; and this baby has already blessed you just by being born. We now increase these blessings with our prayer:

Blessing

(Introduction) God of all creation, we are in your loving care and you have now entrusted this child _____ into the care of these parents _____.

(*Spoken to the infant*)   May you be filled with love, health and happiness. You are welcomed into this family with open hearts and open arms.

(*To the parents*)   May you be filled with all the gifts needed to be outstanding parents, and exercise the privilege and responsibility of parenthood with faithfulness and joy.

(*To parents and baby*)   As a family may you be filled with the fruit and gifts of the Holy Spirit: love and joy, peace and wisdom.

(*Prayer for Protection*)
Christ before you, Christ behind you,
Christ on your left, Christ on your right,
Christ above you, Christ below you,
Christ within you, filling you with life.
(*Alternatives: substitute the title of Christ with God, Peace, Love, or Light.*)

(*May sing this or another song*)
Glory & Praise to Our God (Dan Schutte, S.J.)

Prayer following fetal demise

Baby: _____
Mother: _____
Father: _____

(Farewell Prayer)
God of Gentleness and Love,
You know the sadness and grief these parents
    (and family) are now carrying.
Christ Jesus, Compassionate Consoler,
    at this time, when "hello" also means "goodbye,"
    may these parents *(name)* and *(name)* .
    know that your arms are around them and baby
    (name) .

(Blessing of Parents)
May God's gentleness be with you in your sorrow
    and grant you the peace that passes all
    understanding.

May you feel supported,
    and, in time, raised up from your grief
    and granted the strength and encouragement
    to accept the mysteries of life, death,
        and life-after-death.

(Blessing of Baby)
For this baby (name) :
Eternal rest grant unto *him/her*, O Lord,
    and let perpetual light shine upon *him/her*.
May *he/she* rest in peace.
We trust that *his/her* soul,
    and all the souls of the faithful departed,
    through the mercy of God, rest in peace. Amen.

(Song for the Baby)
May the choirs of angels come to greet you;
May they speed you to paradise.
May the Lord enfold you in his mercy
    as you find eternal life.

(Lord's Prayer)
    Our Father who art in heaven, hallowed be Thy name. Thy kingdom come, Thy will be done on earth as it is in heaven. Give us this day our daily bread, and forgive us our trespasses as we forgive those who trespass against us; and lead us not into temptation but deliver us from evil.

    For thine is the kingdom, the power and the glory, now and forever. Amen.

Pre-op Prayer

A. Fill His/Her Heart with Confidence
(Use of words in parentheses are to be used at the discretion of the minister depending on the patient's faith tradition.)

Let's take a moment to calm our hearts and minds...

Loving and gentle God (heavenly Father and compassionate Mother), graciously protect (*name*) throughout *his/her* surgery. Fill *his/her* heart with confidence so that *he/she* may release anxiety and be filled with peace.

May *his/her* body respond beautifully and perfectly to the surgery and treatment. May *her/his* healing be gentle, swift and thorough.

We pray for the doctor and nurses; fill their minds with wisdom and creative solutions; guide their hands as instruments of healing.

(The minister may invite family members to verbalize a prayer at this time.)

(We pray this in unity with Christ Jesus, the Divine Physician, who knows our sufferings and fears, our needs and longings, and who is here now giving us his divine peace.) Amen.

(Options for Closing:)

1. *Song:* Peace is flowing like a river. (p. 139)

2. Our Father who art in heaven, hallowed be Thy name. Thy kingdom come, Thy will be done on earth as it is in heaven. Give us this day our daily bread, and forgive us our trespasses as we forgive those who trespass against us; and lead us not into temptation but deliver us from evil. For thine is the kingdom, the power and the glory, now and forever. Amen.

3. *Reading from Hebrew scriptures (reprinted in the Jewish section of this manual):*

Ps 91	Angels will guard (p. 14)
Ps 121	Protection (p.16)
Is. 40:28-31	On eagle's wings (p.18)

B. Prayer Before an Operation (Jewish)

Heal us, O Lord, and we shall be healed, save us and we shall be saved; for You are our glory. Grant complete healing for all our afflictions, faithful and merciful God of healing.

Our Creator, who fashioned the human body with all its wonderful complexity, I turn to You in prayer. May the operation I am about to undergo help me return to health. Sustain the surgeon, the nurses and attendants, instruments of Your healing power. Strengthen, O God, my faith in You, so that I may face this ordeal with serenity and with fortitude. Amen.

(Source: Fountain of Life, compiled by Rabbi Arthur A. Chiel and Rabbi Edward T. Sandrow, The Rabbinical Assembly, New York, 1975, p.15. www.ktav.com.)

Post-op Prayer

A. Thanksgiving and Swift Healing

Loving and gracious God, we give you thanks that you have protected _(name)_ during surgery. May _his/her_ healing be swift, comfortable and complete. Enable _him/her_ to trust in your goodness, to find comfort in your abiding presence, and to praise your holy name with joy! (We pray this in unity with Christ Jesus, the Risen One who promises to be ever present in our time of need.) Amen.

(Adapted from Lutheran Occasional Services. Words in parentheses are to be used at the discretion of the minister depending on the patient's faith tradition.)

B. I Thank You that this Operation is Safely Past

O Holy One, we thank you that this operation is safely past. Gently remind _____ _(your son/daughter)_ to relax in Your abiding presence, releasing every tension and care, and receive more and more of Your healing life into every part of _his/her_ being.

If there are moments of pain help *him/her* turn to You for strength; in times of loneliness help *him/her* feel Your loving nearness. May your love and joy flow through *him/her* for the service of others in Your name. Amen.

(Adapted from The Catholic Devotional: A Collection of Prayers and Inspiration for Every Catholic, p.45.)

C. Following an Operation (Jewish)

Avinu Malkeinu, Our Father, Our King, healer of all flesh, I thank You for Your watchful care. Help me to regain my health speedily. Be with me during my recovery. Strengthen me; keep me comfortable and hopeful. Help me to bear all pain with patience and fortitude. May I always be aware of Your comforting presence and always be thankful for Your divine gift of life.

May it be Your will, O Lord our God and God of our fathers, speedily to grant me, and all who lie on beds of pain, perfect healing, the blessed healing of body and soul. Amen.

(Source: Fountain of Life, compiled by Rabbi Arthur A. Chiel and Rabbi Edward T. Sandrow, The Rabbinical Assembly, New York, 1975, p.17. www. ktav.com. Note: Avinu = our Father, Malkeinu = our King.)

Removal of life support

(Said to the unresponsive patient. It is important that the minister speak directly to the unresponsive patient in order to honor the fact that "we are alive until we die," and to model for the family the importance of speaking to their loved one in the last moments. Items in brackets may be omitted based on the patient's religious preference.)

(Name), be at peace now with the knowledge that your task on this earth is nearing its completion. Rest totally in God and surrender into His loving arms.

God has breathed into you the breath of life. Remember that He has carried you from the moment of conception right to this moment, and will continue to do so without end.

[Recall the words of Simeon at the time of Jesus' presentation in the Temple: "Now, Lord, you may let your servant go in peace. Your word has been fulfilled, for my eyes have seen your salvation..."]

[And remember the words of Jesus who, shortly before his death, said, "Father, into your hands I commend my spirit."]

We pray: God, bring your child _(name)_ love and peace at this time. Comfort _her/him_ with the assurance of everlasting life with You.

We pray: Bring your gentle comfort to _his/her_ family. May they know your love and support at this time. May they gently let go and release _(name)_ into your Divine Eternal Light.

(_At this time the minister may invite those gathered to speak loving words to the patient, or verbalize their own prayers._)

(_Optional ending. The minister may select one or another suitable ending:_)

1. Our Father... (pps. 25, 37, 87, or 94)

2. Blessing/Song:
   (Light/Peace/Christ) before you,
   (Light/Peace/Christ) behind you,
   (Light/Peace/Christ) under your feet,
   (Light/Peace/Christ) within you,
   (Light/Peace/Christ) over you,
   let all around you be (Light/Peace/Christ)

3. Blessing/Song:
   We are sending you light for the journey.
   We are sending our peace and our love.
   Trust now that Jesus* will lead you,
   Lead you safely home.
   * or "God"

4. Psalm 23: _The Lord is my Shepherd_ (KJV)
   The Lord is my shepherd; I shall not want. He maketh me to lie down in green pastures; he leadeth me beside

the still waters. He restoreth my soul; he leadeth me in the paths of righteousness for his name's sake.

Yea, though I walk through the valley of the shadow of death, I will fear no evil: for thou art with me; thy rod and thy staff they comfort me.

Thou preparest a table before me in the presence of mine enemies; thou anointest my head with oil; my cup runneth over.

Surely goodness and mercy shall follow me all the days of my life; and I will dwell in the house of the Lord for ever.

5. "Precious Lord" *(found in song section of this manual, p. 140)*

Commendation of the dying

(Spoken to the patient, even if unresponsive: It is important that the minister speak directly to the unresponsive patient in order to honor the fact that "we are alive until we die," and to model for the family the importance of speaking to their loved one in the last moments. Items in brackets may be omitted based on the patient's religious preference.)

We pray: God, bring your child (name) love and peace at this time. *His/Her* journey on this earth is nearly complete. Comfort *him/her* with the assurance of everlasting life with You, and with all those who have gone before and who are now at the heavenly banquet.

(name) , God has breathed into you the breath of life. Remember that He has carried you from the moment of conception right to this moment, and will continue to do so without end.

[Recall the words of Simeon at the time of Jesus' presentation in the Temple; he said: "Now, Lord, you may let your servant go in peace. Your word has been fulfilled, for my eyes have seen your salvation..."]

[And remember the words of Jesus who, shortly before his death, said, "Father, into your hands I commend my spirit."]

(Can place hand on patient, and/or invite family to do same.)

(*Name*), be at peace now with the knowledge of God's total love and acceptance, and that your task on this earth is nearing its completion. Rest totally in God and surrender into His loving arms. Be free to let go of your body and all attachments, and trust that All Shall Be Well.

(At this time the minister may invite those gathered to speak final words to the patient, or verbalize their own prayers.)

[Optional ending. Select one or another suitable ending:]

1. Our Father...

2. Blessing/Song:
   (Light/Peace/Christ) before you,
   (Light/Peace/Christ) behind you,
   (Light/Peace/Christ) under your feet,
   (Light/Peace/Christ) within you,
   (Light/Peace/Christ) over you,
   let all around you be (Light/Peace/Christ)

3. Blessing/Song:
   We are sending you light for the journey.
   We are sending our peace and our love.
   Trust now that Jesus* will lead you,
   Lead you safely home.
   * or "God"

4. Psalm 23: *The Lord is my Shepherd* (KJV)
   The Lord is my shepherd; I shall not want. He maketh

me to lie down in green pastures; he leadeth me beside the still waters. He restoreth my soul; he leadeth me in the paths of righteousness for his name's sake.

Yea, though I walk through the valley of the shadow of death, I will fear no evil: for thou art with me; thy rod and thy staff they comfort me.

Thou preparest a table before me in the presence of mine enemies; thou anointest my head with oil; my cup runneth over.

Surely goodness and mercy shall follow me all the days of my life; and I will dwell in the house of the Lord for ever.

5. "Precious Lord, Take my Hand" (*found in song section, p. 140*).

6. Angels of God surround you,
Lord, send Thy holy angels
to bring Thy comfort and Thy peace
so (he/she) may know your gentle love.
Amen. Amen.

Prayer at the time of death

1. *(Thank God for the life of the one who has died and commend them unto God).*

God, we thank you for the life of _____ *your son/ daughter. His/her* goodness and love will continue to ripple on in the lives of those *he/she* has touched.

2. *(Quotes of comfort)*

We are grateful for the promise of Christ who said, "In the Father's house there are many mansions."

And in Scripture we read, "God is not God of the dead but of the living."

And "To be absent from the body is to be present to the Lord."

We are brought comfort by the thought that even as we on this "shore" of life are saying, "Goodbye, there *he/ she* goes," those on the Far Shore of heaven are greeting *him/her* and saying, "Hello, here *he/she* comes."

We trust, by your mercy, that we will be reunited with our loved ones when you call us Home to heaven.

3. *(Prayers to support family.)*

We offer our prayers for the family. May this season of grief be as gentle as possible.

4. *(Invite family to pray if they so desire.)*

5. *(Song of Commendation)*

I'd now like to sing a song *(or recite the words of an ancient prayer, In Paradisium, In Paradise)* to _____'s soul as we commend *his/her* soul to the care of God through the ministry of the holy angels:

> May the Choirs of Angels come to greet you,
> may they speed you to Paradise;
> May the Lord enfold you in his mercy
> as you find eternal life.

6. *(Lord's Prayer)*

Our Father who art in heaven, hallowed be thy name. Thy kingdom come, thy will be done on earth as it is in heaven. Give us this day our daily bread, and forgive us our trespasses as we forgive those who trespass against us. And lead us not into temptation but deliver us from evil. Amen.

Additional Prayers for the Dying,
Caregivers, the Grieving and the Dead

Prayer for the Dying

Eternal God, you know our needs before we ask,
and you hear our cries through lips unable to speak.
Hear with compassion the yearnings of your servant,
_____, and the prayers that we
would pray had we the words.
Grant *her/him* the assurance of your embrace,
the ears of faith to hear your voice,
and the eyes of hope to see your light.
Release *him/her* from all fear
and from the constraints of life's faults
that *he/she* may breathe *his/her* last
in the peace of your words:
Well done, good and faithful servant;
enter into the joy of your God.
We ask this through Christ our Savior.

Source: United Church of Christ Book of Worship

Prayer for Those Who Care for the Sick

Merciful God, we thank you for all
who minister to _____
in this time of his/her great need.
Give them compassion and tenderness
and the fullest use of their gifts
that they may have the blessed peace
of knowing they honor you
in their acts of healing and comfort.
As death draws near
and there is no more they can do,

let them hear again the words of Jesus Christ:
As often as you did it to one of the least of these,
you did it to me;
and fill them with the joy of your Holy Spirit. Amen.

Source: United Church of Christ Book of Worship

Prayer for the Grieving
Great God of all mystery,
if in the presence of death our thoughts are startled
and our words flutter about like frightened birds,
bring us stillness
that we may cover the sorrow
of our hearts with folded hands.
Give us grace to wait on your silently and with patience.
You are nearer to us than we know,
closer than we can imagine.
If we cannot find you, it is because we search in far places.
Before we felt the pain, you suffered it;
before the burden came upon us, your strength lifted it;
before the sorrow darkened our hearts, you were grieved.
As you walk in the valley of every shadow,
be our Good Shepherd
and sustain us as we walk with you,
lest in weakness we falter.
Though the pain deepens, keep us in your way
and guide us past every danger;
through Jesus Christ our Savior. Amen.

Source: Adapted from Prayers for Daily Use by Samuel H. Miller
(Harper & Row, 1957), p. 128.

Commendation at the Time of Death

Depart, O Christian *sister/brother*
out of this world:
in the name of God most holy, who created you;
in the name of Jesus Christ, who redeemed you;
in the name of the Holy Spirit, who sanctifies you.
May you rest this *day/night*
in the peace of God's eternal home. Amen.

Source: Adapted from the 1979 Episcopal Book of Common Prayer.

Commendation at the Time of Death 2

Into your hands, O merciful Savior,
we commend your servant _____.
Acknowledge, we humbly pray, a sheep of your own fold,
a lamb of your own flock,
and a *son/daughter* of your own redeeming.
Receive *him/her* into the arms of your mercy,
into the blessed rest of everlasting peace,
and into the company of the saints in light. Amen.

Source: Adapted from the 1979 Episcopal Book of Common Prayer.

Quotes of hope on the topic of death

Requiescat in pace. (Latin)
Translation: Rest in peace.

Eternal rest grant unto *him/her*, O Lord,
and let perpetual light shine upon *him/her*.
May *he/she* rest in peace. Amen.

Vita mutatur, non tollitur (Latin)
Translation: Life changes but is not destroyed.

There, She is Gone (And That is Dying)
*(Variously attributed to Rev. Luther F. Beecher
or Henry Van Dyke)*

I am standing on the seashore. A ship at my side
spreads her white sails to the morning breeze and
starts for the blue ocean. She is an object of beauty and
strength. I stand and watch her until at length she hangs
like a speck of white cloud just where the sea and sky
come to mingle with eachother.

Then someone at my side says, "There, she is gone!"

"Gone where?"

Gone from my sight. That is all. She is just as large in mast and hull and spar as she was when she left my side; and she is just as able to bear her load of freight to her destined port.

Her diminished size is in me, not in her. And just at the moment when someone at my side says, "There, she is gone!" there are other eyes watching her coming, and other voices ready to take up the glad shout: "Here she comes!"

And that is dying.

Death is Nothing at All.
(Henry Scott Holland, 1847-1918,
Canon of St. Paul's Cathedral, London)

Death is nothing at all. I have only slipped away to the next room. I am I, and you are you. Whatever we were to each other, that we still are.

Call me by my old familiar name. Speak to me in the easy way which you always used. Put no difference into your tone. Wear no forced air of solemnity or sorrow.

Laugh as we always laughed at the little jokes we enjoyed together. Play, smile, think of me, pray for me. Let my name be ever the household word that it always was. Let it be spoken without effect, without the trace of a shadow on it.

Life means all that it ever meant. It is the same that it ever was. There is absolute unbroken continuity. Why should I be out of mind because I am out of sight? I am but waiting for you, for an interval, somewhere very near, just around the corner.

All is well.

PART 4

BIBLICAL RESOURCES: TOPICAL LISTINGS

Where to find encouragement when...

Afraid
       Ps 91   Dwell in God's shelter
       Lk 8:22-25   Jesus calms the storm
       1 Jn 4:18   Perfect love casts out fear

Afraid (persecuted)
       Ps 6   Prayer when in distress
       Ps 118:5-6   In anguish I cried to the Lord
       Is 41:10   Don't be afraid, I am with you
       Mt 5:11-12   When insulted
       Mt 10:26-28   When under persecution
       Hb 13:6   The Lord is my helper
       2 Tm 1:7   Did not give a spirit of timidity

Anxious
       Is 26:3   Peace —thoughts fixed on God
       Is 41:10   Don't be afraid, I am with you

Is 43:21	will be with you
Mt 6:25-34	Lilies of the field
Mt 11:28-30	Come to me all who are weary
Jn 14:1	Don't let your heart be troubled
Jn 14:27	Peace I leave you
2 Cor 1:3-5	God of comfort
Phil 4:4-7	Have no anxiety
1 Pt 5:7	Cast all your cares upon God

Bereaved (Death of loved one)

Is 51:11	Sorrow will disappear
Is 53:4	He has borne our griefs
Mt 5:4	Blessed are sorrowful
Mt 11:28-29	Come to me all who labor
Jn 11:25	I am the resurrection
Jn 14:1-4	Many mansions
1 Cor 15:26	Death is destroyed
1 Cor 15:51-55	Where is sting

Depressed

Neh 8:10	Don't be sad, joy is your strength
Ps 42:2-12	As the deer longs
Ps 118:24	This is the day the Lord has made
Is 40:31	Soar like eagle, not be weary
Phil 4:8-9	Whatever is true...

(Facing) Death

Ps 23	The Lord is my Shepherd
1 Thes 4:16	The dead in Christ will rise
Rev 21:4	Wipe every tear; no more death

Discouraged

Is 40:29	He gives power to the weak
Is 40:31	Soar like eagle, not be weary
Phil 4:4-7	Rejoice in the Lord
1 Pt 5:7	Cast all your cares upon God

Facing a Crisis

Ps 121	Not allow foot to slip
Is 41:10	Don't be afraid, I am with you
Mt 6:25-34	Lilies of field
Rom 8:31, 37-39	God is for us
Hb 4:16	Find timely help

Forgiveness

Lk 5:17-26	Heal and forgive the paralytic

Healing (see next section, p. 118)

Lamenting

Ps 88	A despairing lament

Seeking Truth

Pr 3:5-6	Trust in the Lord
Pr 4:6-9	Esteem wisdom

Seeking Wisdom
        Ps 119:109   Thy word is lamp
        Job 28:20-21,23-24 Hidden Wisdom
Weary
        Mt 11:28-30   Come to me all who are weary
Worried
        Matt 6:25-34   Birds of the air
        1 Pt 5:6-7   Cast all your cares
(Wanting to) Worship
        Rev 5:11-14   Worthy is the Lamb

Encouragement when Seeking...

Courage

	Ps 46	Refuge, ever present help
	Is 41:10	Don't be afraid, I am with you
	Jn 16:33	I have overcome the world
	Heb 13:6	I will not be afraid
	2 Tim 1:17	Not a spirit of fear

Encouragement

	2 Cor 1:3-4	God encourages us
	2 Cor 12:8-10	Grace sufficient
Faith	Is 40:31	They that wait upon the Lord
	Mt 17:20	Mustard seed

Guidance

	Ps 32:8-11	I will instruct you
	Mt 7:24-27	House on rock
	Jn 16:13	Spirit of truth guides
	Hb 4:16	Approach throne
	Jm 1:5-6	Ask for wisdom

Healing

Pss. 3, 6, 13, 16, 20, 23, 30, 32, 38, 39, 41, 42, 59, 77, 90, 105, 121, 137, 150.

Ps 147:3	He heals the broken-hearted
Lk 5:12-26	Healing of leper and paralytic

Hope

Rom 8:28, 38-39	All things work for good

Humility

Jam 4:13-15	Life is a mist

Joy

Neh 8:10	The joy of the L is strength.
Ps 16:11	In Your presence is full joy
Ps 100	Make a joyful noise
Ps 118:24	This is the day the Lord made
Phil 4:4	Rejoice in Lord always

Peace and Hope

Jn 14:1	Do not be disturbed
Jn 16:33	Have peace in me
Phil 4:6-7	Have no anxiety

Positive Attitude

Phil 4:8-9	Whatever is true...

Protection by God

Ps 91	My refuge and fortress
Is 41:10	Don't be afraid, I am with you

Rest

Ps 23	Lord is my shepherd

Guidance on living

Changing one's ways

Ezek 36:26	New heart, stony heart to flesh
Rom 12:2	Renewing of mind
Eph 4:21-24	Put old self away

Commitment to God

Ps 37:5	Commit your way

Discipline of God

Hb 12:5-6	The Lord disciplines

Follow Law of Lord

Ps 1	Don't follow bad counsel

Forgiveness

Ps 51	Wash away my guilt
Mt 5:38-42	Eye for an eye
Jn 8:7	First to throw a stone
Col 3:12-15	Clothe self with love, forgive

Gratitude

1 Thes 5:18	In everything give thanks

Guidance for Living
    Mt 5:3-12   Beatitudes
    Rom 12   Offer bodies as sacrifice
Judging others
    Mt 7:1-5   Plank in eye
Love one another
    Mt 7:12   Golden Rule
    Lk 6:27-38   Love enemies
    Lk 10:27   Love God & Neighbor
    Jn 13:34-35   Love one another
    1 Cor 13   Love is patient
    1 Jn 4:7-8 & 11   Love
    Col 3:12-17   Clothe w/ compassion,
                             forgive

Money
    1 Tim 6:10   love of money
Pride   1 Jn 2:16   Boasting is not
                             of the Father

Priorities
    Mt 6:19-21   Treasure in heavn
    Lk 10:27   Love God and neighbor
Salvation
    Rom 8:1   No condemnation
Temple of the Holy Spirit
    1 Cor 6:19-20   Body is temple
Temptation
    Jam 1:12-16   persevere

Sacraments

Baptism   Mt 28:19   Baptize in the name of
Eucharist   Mt 26:26-28   This is my body

Virtues, Values, Misc.

Faith	Heb 11:	Faith of the ancients
Fruit of Spirit		
	Gal 5:22-23	Fruit of the Spirit
God's knows us		
	Ps 139	You have formed me
Identity as a human		
	Mt 5:14-16	Light of the world
	Lk 17:21	Kingdom of God is within
	Phil 3:20	Citizenship in heaven
	Phil 1:21	To live is Christ
	Phil 2:12	God is at work in you
Jesus is present		
	Mt 4:16	Seen a great light
	Mt 18:20	Where two or three
	Jn 4:4	Living water
	Jn 7:37-38	If anyone thirsts...
	Jn 10:27-28	My sheep hear my voice
	Jn 15:4-6	I am the vine
	Rev 3:20	I stand at the door

Kingdom of God
        Mt 18:12-14   Lost sheep
Lost & Found
        Lk 15   Lost sheep, prodigal son
Mystery
        1 Cor 2:9-10   Eye has not seen
Paradox
        Mk 8:35-36   Save life will lose it
Praise & Thanksgiving
        Ps 34:1-11   I will bless the Lord
        Ps 100   Shout joyfully
Prayer   Ps 42   As the deer longs
        Mt 6:5-8   When you pray
        Mt 7:7-8   Ask, it will be given
        Mt 18:20   Where two or three are
                             gatherd
        Mt 21:22   Whatever you ask
        Lk 11:1-13   Teaching on prayer
        1 Thes 5:17   Pray w/o ceasing
        1 Jn 5:14-15   Ask according to his will
Thanksgiving
        1 Th 5:18   Give thanks always

Psalms, Topically

Afraid
     Ps 91   Dwell in God's shelter

Afraid (when persecuted)
     Ps 6   Prayer in distress
     Ps 118:5-6   In danger I called

Angels
     Ps 91

Commit to God
     Ps 37:5   Commit your way

Courage
     Ps 46   Refuge, ever present
help

Depressed
     Ps 42:2-12   As the deer longs
     Ps 118:24   This is the day

Facing a Crisis
     Ps 121   Not allow foot to slip

Forgiveness
     Ps 51   Wash away my guilt

God knows us

Ps 139   You have formed me

Guidance

Ps 32:8-11   I will instruct you

Healing

Pss. 3, 6, 13, 16, 20, 23, 30, 32, 38, 39, 41, 42,
59, 77, 90, 105, 121, 137, 150.

Joy   Ps 16:11   You will fill me with joy

Ps 28:7   My strength and shield

Ps 100   Make a joyful noise

Ps 118:24   This is the day

Lament

Ps 88   A despairing lament

Law of Lord

Ps 1   Don't follow bad counsel

Ps 119:109   Thy word is lamp

Praise & Thanksgiving

Ps 34:1-11   I will bless the Lord

Ps 100   Shout joyfully, praise his
name

Prayerful

Ps 42   As the deer longs

Protection

Ps 91   My refuge and fortress

Rest   Ps 23   Lord is my shepherd

Select passages as ordered in the Bible

Some Favorite Stories in the Jewish Scriptures (TANAK)

Creation	Gen 1
Adam & Eve	Gen 2:4
Noah's Ark	Gen 6
Abraham	Gen 12
Hagar & Ishmael	Gen 16
Sacrifice of Isaac	Gen 22
Jacob's dream of stairway/ladder	Gen 28:10
Jacob wrestles angel, renamed Israel	Gen 32:22
Joseph's dream of sheaves of grain	Gen 37:5
Moses and burning bush	Ex 3
Passover	Ex 12:23
The Exodus	Ex 12:33
Ten Commandments	Ex 20, Deut 5
"Hear, O Israel" (summary of Law)	Deut 6:4-9
The call to Samuel ("Here I am")	1 Sam 3
David anointed	1 Sam 16:12
David & Goliath	1 Sam 17:32

David & Bathsheba	2 Sam 11
Solomon's wise judgment re. child	1 Kng 3:16
Solomon builds the Temple	1 Kng 6
The widow's oil and flour	1 Kng 17:7
Elijah vs Baal's prophets on Mt Carmel	1 Kng 18:20
Elijah taken to heaven in whirlwind	2 Kng 2
Naaman cured of leprosy	2 Kng 5
God's answer to Job's complaints	Job 38
"Vanity of vanities!"	Eccl. 1
"There is a time for everything"	Eccl 3
Ezekial's vision of valley of dry bones	Ez 37
Daniel in lion's den	Dan 6:16
What does the Lord require?	Micah 6:8

Additional favorite passages in Jewish scriptures

Deut 30:15-20	Choose life and live
Neh 8:10	Don't be sad, joy of L is your strength
Job 28:20-21,23-24	Hidden Wisdom
Pr 3:5-6	Trust in the Lord
Pr 4:6-9	Esteem wisdom
Is 26:3	Peace —thoughts fixed on God
Is 40:29	He gives power to the weak
Is 40:31	Soar like eagle, not be weary
Is 41:10	Don't be afraid, I am with you
Is 43:2	I will be with you
Is 51:11	Sorrow will disappear
Ezek 36:26	New heart, stony heart to flesh

Psalms, as Ordered, with Topical Theme

Ps 1	Don't follow bad counsel	*:Law of Lord*
Ps 6	Prayer in distress	*:Persecuted*
Ps 23	Lord is my shepherd	*:Rest*
Ps 32:8-11	I will instruct you	*:Guidance*
Ps 34:1-11	I will bless the L	*:Praise/Thank*
Ps 37:5	Commit your way	*:Commitment*
Ps 42:2-12	As the deer longs	*:Rest in God*
Ps 46	Refuge, help	*:Courage*
Ps 51	Wash away my guilt	*:Forgiveness*
Ps 88	A despairing lament	*:Lament*
Ps 91	My refuge and fortress	*:Security*
Ps 100	Make a joyful noise	*:Joy*
Ps 118:5-6	In danger I called	*:Persecuted*
Ps 118:24	This is the day	*:Rejoice*
Ps 119:109	Thy word is lamp	*:Law of Lord*
Ps 121	Not allow foot to slip	*:Security*
Ps 139	You have formed me	*:God knows us*
Ps 147:3	Heals the broken-heart	*:Grief*
Pss, Healing:	3, 6, 13, 16, 20, 23, 30, 32, 38, 39, 41, 42, 59, 77, 90, 105, 121, 137, 150.	

New Testament
Select Passages

Mt 4:16	Seen a great light
Mt 5-7	Sermon on the Mount
Mt 5:3-12	Beatitudes
Mt 5:14-16	Light of the world
Mt 5:38-42	Eye for an eye
Mt 6:5-13	When you pray, Lord's Prayer
Mt 6:19-21	Treasure in heaven
Mt 6:25-34	Birds of air, Lilies of the field
Mt 6:33	Seek ye first the kingdom of God
Mt 7:1-5	Plank in eye
Mt 7:7-8	Ask, it will be given
Mt 7:12	Golden Rule
Mt 7:24-27	Build house on rock
Mt 10:26-28	Under persecution
Mt 11:28-30	Come to me all who are weary
Mt 17:20	Mustard seed
Mt 18:12-14	Lost sheep
Mt 18:20	Where two or three are gathered
Mt 21:22	Whatever you ask
Mt 26:26-28	This is my body (Eucharist)

Mk 8:35-36	Save life will lose it
Lk 1:37	With God nothing is impossible
Lk 5:17-26	Heal and forgive the paralytic
Lk 6:27-38	Love enemies
Lk 8:22-25	Jesus calms storm
Lk 8:42-48	Woman with hemorrhage
Lk 10:27	Love God and neighbor
Lk 11:1-13	Teaching on prayer, "Lord's Prayer"
Lk 15	Lost sheep, prodigal son
Lk 17:21	Kingdom of God is within
Jn 3:16	For God so loved the world
Jn 4:4	Living water
Jn 7:37-38	If anyone thirsts
Jn 8:7	First to throw a stone
Jn 10:27-28	My sheep hear my voice
Jn 11:25	I am the Resurrection
Jn 13:34-35	Love one another
Jn 14:1-4	Don't be troubled, Many mansions
Jn 14:27	Peace I leave you
Jn 15:4-6	I am the vine
Jn 16:13	Spirit of truth guides
Jn 16:33	Peace, I have overcome world
Rom 8:28, 31, 37-39	All things work together for good
Rom 12	Offer bodies as sacrifice
Rom 12:2	Renewing of mind
1 Cor 2:9-10	Eye has not seen
1 Cor 6:19-20	Body is a temple of the Holy Spirit
1 Cor 10:13	Temptation
1 Cor 13	Love is patient, Love is kind
1 Cor 15:26	Death destroyed
1 Cor 15:51-55	O death, where is thy sting?
2 Cor 1:3-5	God of comfort encourages us

2 Cor 12:8-10	My grace is sufficient
Gal 5:22-23	Fruit of the Holy Spirit
Eph 4:21-24	Put old self away
Phil 1:21	To live is Christ, to die is gain
Phil 2:12	God is at work in you
Phil 3:20	Citizenship in heaven
Phil 4:4-7	Have no anxiety, rejoice
Phil 4:8-9	Whatever is true, lovely, noble
Col 3:12-17	Clothe w/ compassion, forgive
1 Thes 4:16	The dead in Christ will rise
1 Thes 5:17-18	Pray w/o ceasing, give thanks
1 Tim 6:10	Love of money
2 Tm 1:7	Not a spirit of cowardice
Heb 4:16	Approach throne, find timely help
Heb 11	Faith of the Ancients
Heb 12:5-6	The Lord disciplines
Heb 13:6	The L is my helper, I will not be afraid
Jam 1:5-6	Ask for wisdom
Jam 1:12-16	Persevere
Jam 4:13-15	Life is a mist
1 Pet 5:6-7	Cast all your cares upon God
1 Jn 2:16	The pride of life
1 Jn 5:14-15	Ask according to his will
1 Jn 4:7-8 & 11	Beloved, let us love one another
Rev 3:20	I stand at the door and knock
Rev 5:11-14	(Worship) Worthy is the Lamb
Rev 21:4	Wipe every tear; no more death

PART 5

SONGS

Amazing grace

(One of Christianity's most beloved hymns. Lyrics by John Newton, 1779, once a sailor participating in the slave trade, later had a conversion and was ordained in the Church of England)

1. Amazing Grace, how sweet the sound
   That saved a wretch like me.
   I once was lost but now am found,
   Was blind, but now I see.

2. T'was Grace that taught my heart to fear.
   And Grace, my fears relieved.
   How precious did that Grace appear
   The hour I first believed.

3. Through many dangers, toils and snares
   I have already come;
   'Tis Grace that brought me safe thus far
   and Grace will lead me home.

4. The Lord has promised good to me.
   His word my hope secures.
   He will my shield and portion be,
   As long as life endures.

5. When we've been here ten thousand years
   Bright shining as the sun.
   We've no less days to sing God's praise
   Than when we've first begun.

How Great Thou Art

(A Protestant favorite, inspired by a poem by Carl Boberg, Sweden 1885, translation and additional verses by Stuart Hine, Methodist missionary.)

1. O Lord my God, when I in awesome wonder, consider all the worlds thy hands have made; I see the stars I hear the rolling thunder; thy power throughout the universe displayed.

Refrain: Then sings my soul, my savior God to thee.
    How great thou art! (2x)

2. When through the woods, and forest glades I wander, and hear the birds sing sweetly in the trees. When I look down, from loft mountain grandeur and see the brook, and feel the gentle breeze.

3. When Christ shall come, with shout of acclamation, and take me home, what joy shall fill my heart. Then I shall bow, in humble adoration, and then proclaim, "My God, how great thou art!"

It is Well with my Soul

*(Horatio Spafford, 1873. Written following the
tragic death of his four daughters in a shipwreck.)*

When peace like a river attendeth my way,
When sorrows like sea billows roll,
Whatever my lot Thou hast taught me to say,
"It is well, it is well with my soul."
It is well with my soul.
It is well, it is well with my soul!

Peace is Flowing Like a River

(Traditional)

Peace is flowing like a river,
flowing out of you and me,
flowing out into the desert,
setting all the captives free.

Precious Lord

(Thomas A. Dorsey, 1932. Baptist minister.
Written in response to his grief following the deaths of his wife,
Nettie Harper, in childbirth, and his infant son.)

1. Precious Lord, take my hand, lead me on, let me stand. I am tired I am weak, I am worn. Through the storm, through the night, lead me on to the light. Take my hand, precious Lord, lead me Home.

2. When my way grows drear, precious Lord, linger near. When my life is almost gone. Hear my cry, hear my call, hold my hand lest I fall. Take my hand, precious Lord, lead me home.

3. When the darkness appears and the night draws near, and the day is past and gone, at the River I stand, guide my feet, hold my hand; take my hand, precious Lord, lead me home.

The Priestly Blessing
(Jewish. Num 6:24-26)

The Lord bless you and keep you!
The Lord make his face to shine upon you
    and be gracious unto you.
The Lord lift up his countenance
    and look upon you
And grant you peace! Amen, amen.

(Sheet music available at
www.apocryphile.org/imh.html)

We are sending you light for the journey
Matt Sanders

We are sending you light for the journey
We are sending our peace and our love.
Trust now that Jesus* will lead you,
Lead you safely home.

*God

(Sheet music available at
www.apocryphile.org/imh.html)

Angels of God Surround You

Matt Sanders

Angels of God surround you,
Lord, send Thy holy angels
to bring Thy comfort *(healing)* and Thy peace
so *(he/she)* may know your gentle love.
Amen. Amen.

(Sheet music available at
www.apocryphile.org/imh.html)

PART 6

OTHER RESOURCES

12 Steps of AA

1. We admitted we were powerless over alcohol— that our lives had become unmanageable.

2. Came to believe a Power greater than ourselves could restore us to sanity.

3. Made a decision to turn our wills and our lives over to the care of God, *as we understood Him.*

4. Made a searching and fearless moral inventory of ourselves.

5. Admitted to God, to ourselves, and to another human being the exact nature of our wrongs.

6. Were entirely ready to have God remove all these defects of character.

7. Humbly asked Him to remove our shortcomings.

8. Made a list of all persons we had harmed, and became willing to make amends to them all.

9. Made direct amends to such people wherever possible, except when to do so would injure them or others.

10. Continued to take personal inventory and when we were wrong promptly admitted it.

11. Sought through prayer and meditation to improve our conscious contact with God, *as we understood Him*, praying only for knowledge of His will for us and the power to carry that out.

12. Having had a spiritual awakening as a result of these Steps, we tried to carry this message to other alcoholics, and to practice these principles in all our affairs.

"Without this Faith" by Helen Keller

*(Helen Keller, 1880-1968, fell ill at nineteen
months of age and lost sight and hearing.)*

Without this faith there would be little meaning in my life. I should be "a mere pillar of darkness in the dark."

Observers in the full enjoyment of their bodily senses pity me, but it is because they do not see the golden chamber in my life where I dwell delighted; for, dark as my path may seem to them, I carry a magic light in my heart.

Faith, the spiritual strong searchlight, illumines the way, and although sinister doubts lurk in the shadow, I walk unafraid toward the Enchanted Wood where the foliage is always green, where joy abides, where nightingales nest and sing, and where life and death are one in the presence of the Lord.

Helen Keller on Handicaps:

"I thank God for my handicaps, for, through them, I have found myself, my work and my God."

MCR: Mind Controlled Relaxation

(Based on the work of motivational speaker Ed Foreman, www.edforeman.com. Permission granted. This is an effective relaxation process for others when the setting and timing is appropriate. It is recommended to record the process and reap its benefits for oneself before attempting to use it with others. Modify it as needed based on circumstances. Step 15 allows for customization of what is needed in relaxation. Ask the patient what they need such as better sleep, release of worries, release of pain, and healing; then offer these hopes in the form of positive affirmations during step 15.)

1. Sit or lay comfortably on a recliner, couch or bed.

2. Gently stretch your body. And relax.

3. When I say "raise" hold up your head & shoulders and your feet about 4 inches, until the count of twelve. Ready: raise. 1, 2, 3, 4, 5, 6, 7, 8, 9, 10, 11, 12. And relax.

4. Now imagine yourself standing at the top of a long escalator. Place your hand on the handrail, step onto the top step. Count down from 10, 9, 8, 7, 6, 5, 4, 3, 2, 1 and zero.

5. Step off the escalator, and step over to the top of another long escalator. Place your hand on the handrail, step onto the top step. Count down from 10, 9, 8, 7, 6, 5, 4, 3, 2, 1 and zero.

6. Step off the escalator, and step over to another way-down-deep escalator. Place your hand on the handrail, step onto the top step. Count down from 10, 9, 8, 7, 6, 5, 4, 3, 2, 1 and zero.

7. Walk out onto a beautiful opening of a carpet of soft green grass. Imagine yourself lying there, on a big blanket, so comfortable and peaceful.

8. See a fluffy white cloud floating lazily along above you. It's so easy to imagine yourself lying on that soft, fluffy cloud, sinking deeper and deeper into the cloud, and into relaxation, letting go of all tension and tightness.

9. In a moment I will ask you to inhale a nice big breath of good, clean, oxygen-filled air. Ready?
    Inhale—Hold it—Slowly release through the mouth: 3, 3, 3, 3, 3...
    Once again: Inhale—Hold it—Slowly release through the mouth: 2, 2, 2, 2, 2...
    One more time, this time inhaling the biggest and deepest breath of air: Inhale—Hold it—Slowly release through the mouth: 1, 1, 1, 1, 1...

10. You feel so relaxed, tension-free, at peace and at ease.

11. Now imagine your favorite place of relaxation.
    You may imagine yourself lying on a warm, sandy beach. Feel the heat of the sun on your skin; taste the salty air on your lips; feel the gentle breeze of the ocean.
    Or imagine you're in a cozy mountain cabin, all bundled up, resting lazily in a recliner; a fire is crackling in the fireplace, while large flakes of snow are falling outside the window.
    Or imagine sitting before a calm mountain lake. See the ripples of the water settle into a still, glassy surface; the reflection of the mountain and clouds can be seen on the lake. Everything is so peaceful.

12. On the count of 5 you will feel the peace, happiness, and calmness as if you were actually there. 1, 2, 3, 4, 5!

13. You're so relaxed from the tip of your toes to the top of your head.
Your toes are so relaxed,
feet, heels, ankles are relaxed,
calves, knees, thighs, hips,
back—totally, beautifully relaxed and tension free.
stomach, chest,
all muscles and organs,
fingers, hands, forearms,
neck, face, head—totally relaxed.

14. With each breath you will think
deep (in) sleep (out). And deep (in) sleep (out)...

15. I will now count down from 50 to 0. I will offer various affirmations and positive suggestions. You might fall asleep before I reach zero. That's perfectly fine.
(The affirmations can be tailor-fit for the person based on your conversation before the exercise began.)
50, 49, 48...Resting, relaxing...resting, relaxing.
47, 46, 45...Deep, sleep...deep, sleep.
44, 43, 42...Resting, relaxing...resting, relaxing.
41, 40, 39, 38 ...Beautifully relaxed from the crown of your head to the souls of your feet.
37, 36, 35...Deep, sleep...deep, sleep.
34, 33, 32...Your brain is resting, calming, quietly rejuvenating.
31, 30, 29, 28...Your lungs and heart are working beautifully well. Breathing in good, clean, oxygen-filled air. Pumping healthy blood throughout the body.

27, 26, 25...Your sense of inner peace is growing and expanding. All shall be well. You understand more and more deeply that all is well.

24, 23, 22...Your mind opens up to all positivity and goodness. Your mind is filled with light and love. Light, love. Light and love.

21, 20, 19, 18... Your kidneys and liver are functioning so well, purifying the blood as it circulates throughout the body.

17, 16, 15... Resting, relaxing...resting, relaxing.

14, 13, 12...Way-down-deep peace; deep, sleep.

11, 10, 9... Calm. Happy, healthy, terrific.

8, 7, 6...Calm. Happy, healthy, terrific.

5, 4...Deep, sleep; deep sleep.

3, 2, 1, zero.

(Quietly exit the room at this time. Of course explain prior to the beginning of the exercise that you intend to slip out of the room silently without saying goodbye at the end.)

– THOUGHTS ON PRAYER –

A. On Healings by Matt Sanders

Some healing is spontaneous and indeed miraculous in the true sense of that word. Usually, however, healing is gradual and one ought not be discouraged by the slowness of the healing process. Being patient amidst the slowness of healing will in itself bring healings of other kinds.

There are different kinds and degrees of healing:

Healing of body. This may include a continuance of the physical ailment itself but an increased relaxation around the suffering. An increased acceptance of that which we cannot change tends to support the healing process.

Psychological healing. This includes emotions, memory, attitudes, will, or an individual's distinctive and unique thought process itself. One may be given the immense gift of recognizing the subtle workings of one's own mind; a person may see that he or she is continually creating thoughts and those thoughts are creating their experience of life. One may shift toward a deeper sense of awareness, detachment, and acceptance.

Spiritual healing. This may include a healing of one's relationship with oneself whereby a person relaxes into a peaceful self-acceptance, acceptance of their powerlessness and recognition of their gifts. A person may heal in their moral and ethical commitment. Healing may come in one's relationship with the Divine and core spiritual orientation, and experience an enlightenment or a born-anew experience. Fear may be transformed into trust; despair may be transformed into hope; hate may be dissolved by forgiveness; sadness may grow into joy; worry may be replaced by a peace that passes all understanding; confusion may give way to vision; depression may be replaced by a love of life and vibrant creativity; complacency may be replaced by a joyful commitment and energy for self-care and balance; lust may be replaced by healthy sexuality; ego may loosen its grip while humble humor grows; vanity may be replaced by humility and love. Disregard for others may be replaced by profound compassion and sensitivity to the feelings of people and animals; prejudice may be burned up like dross, leaving a purity of the simple acceptance of others; dishonesty may be replaced by a commitment to truth and integrity.

Healing of relationships. During a time of physical illness, psychological crisis, financial ruin, or imprisonment, a person may, potentially, find the healing of key relationships. Crises may strain or tear apart relationships so a minister may find it important to assist patients and families explore ways to nurture relationships, forgive, recommit to one another, and keep promises; the chaplain may be a key advocate in helping individuals and families find resources that can be of support during times of stress, change and crisis. Healing may come in the form of a patient or family finding greater clarity and courage to advocate for their own needs. The minister may help provide a "reframing," a fresh perspective so a family may recognize that the healing of relationships is one of the healing gifts for which to give thanks and praise.

The minister may find it appropriate to encourage patients and families to be open to the multiple and unpredictable ways that healing may come. Allow oneself to be surprised by the unpredictable manner in which healing shows up. Don't cling to a particular expectation. Notice and celebrate every healing, no matter how small. The chaplain is in the privileged role of being able to look carefully at a person's life, to listen carefully to their story, and then to shine a spotlight on the good. Exercise your gift of encouragement and *name* the good, the gifts, and the healings you see. We may be able to assist a person to perceive more clearly the multiple healings that are happening and thus help them to reframe their circumstances into a more hopeful view of life.

B. Healthy Prayer and Neurotic Prayer
(By Joan Chittister. The Breath of the Soul: Reflections on Prayer. Twenty-Third Publications, 2009)

"Healthy prayer and neurotic prayer are two different things. Neurotic prayer denies reality. Healthy prayer grows both spiritually and psychologically as a result of it.

"When we fail to accept the fact that some things just are: that rain rains and sickness comes and the unexpected is commonplace – when we fail to realize that life is life, all of it meant to teach us something, to give new opportunities to be better, stronger people – we miss both the meaning of life and the real role of prayer in it.

"The spiritually mature person does not rely on God for miracles. They rely on God for strength and courage, for insight and hope, for vision and endurance. They know that God is with them; they do not believe that God is an instrument for the comfort of human beings.

"They do know that one of the purposes of prayer is to give them the courage it takes to do what we are each meant to do in the world that is ours. They do not forgive themselves the responsibility for changing their own little piece of the world on the grounds that if they pray hard enough God will change the world for them. They know that, without doubt, it is their responsibility to change the world."

C. From Rabbi Nahman of Bratslav
(As quoted in The Wings of the Sun: Traditional Jewish Healing in Theory and Practice, by Avraham Greenbaum, pp. 382-422):

1. By Lubavitcher Rebbe, Refuah Shelemah, A Complete Healing, p.57:
"Instead of focusing on the illness, contemplate something that will bring you to a state of joy, such as the thought with which we are all asked to begin each day, 'Modeh ani lefanekha' 'I gratefully thank You in Your Presence, Spirit of Radiant Life, enduring.' Focus on the fact that you are constantly before the Divine Presence."

2. From Talmud, Bava Metzia 30b:
"Whoever visits the sick removes 1/60 of their suffering."

D. Mevlana Jalaluddin Rumi, 13th c.
What is praised is One so the praise is one too,
    many jugs being poured into a huge basin.
All religions, all this singing—one song.
        The differences are just illusion and vanity.
Sunlight looks slightly different on this wall
    than it does on that wall and a lot different

on this other one, but it is still one light.
We have borrowed these clothes,
  these time-and-space personalities, from a Light,
  and when we praise, we pour them back in.

E. Padre Pio

"A lady asked (Padre Pio) what prayers were most acceptable to God. (Padre Pio) replied: 'All prayers are good, when these are accompanied by the right intention and good will.'"
(Padre Pio: The Stigmatist, Fr. Charles Mortimer Carty, TAN Books and Publishers, Inc., 1973, p. 234.)

F. Healing Prayer, Francis MacNutt

In *The Practice of Healing Prayer: A How-To Guide for Catholics* (The Word Among Us Press, 2010, p. 23) Francis MacNutt says to pray with expectant faith that you will see astounding healings done by God when you believe and pray. Have confidence that anyone can pray for healing—not just "holy people". And when you pray for healing don't just pray at a distance, also pray with the sick person, with a laying on of hands if that is appropriate. And teach families to pray for their loved ones in this way.

MacNutt elsewhere has said that we don't know how or when healing will come, but we do know God loves us, that he hears our prayers, and that there are different kinds of healings, so be open to what may come.

G. Rabbi Abraham Heschel

"Just to be is a blessing. Just to live is holy."

H. Huston Smith on Hinduism:

"Early on, the Vedas announced Hinduism's classic contention that the various religions are but different languages through which God speaks to the human heart. 'Truth is one; sages call it by different names.'" (*The World's Religions p. 73.*)

Ordination Vows
The Chaplaincy Institute

*The following are vows that were taken by the ordinands of the
Chaplaincy Institute, Berkeley, CA, March 19, 2011.*

I vow to honor the Divine and deepen my awareness of
Spirit in all its manifest and unmanifest forms.

I will honor my mind, body and spirit as sacred vessels
of grace.

I will seek, serve, and celebrate the spark of divinity
within all beings.

I will carry the spirit of Interfaith awareness wherever
my ministry takes me and create bridges of understanding
and respect between people of different faith traditions.

I will keep sacred my ethical responsibilities as an
Interfaith Minister.

I will work to achieve a peaceful, just and sustainable
world.

I will hold as holy all of Creation, promoting balance
and harmony within the web of life.

Index

People

Bible Passages

If you found this book helpful, please consider reading:

Death is inevitable, mysterious, and often confusing.

At the deathbed, patients and those gathered seek meaning, and many long for a sense of the Spiritual. Yet chaplains and spiritual caregivers have minimal information by which to determine how to provide support, limited time to develop rapport, and varying expectations from those they serve.

Regardless of the religious background of the patient and the loved ones gathered at the deathbed, there are elements of symbol and ritual that take on a pronounced role and a greater importance as one is facing the end of life.

Available wherever paperbacks are sold.
ISBN 978-1-944769-66-6

Made in the USA
Monee, IL
12 April 2021